The ANC and the Liberation Struggle

The ANC and the Liberation Struggle

A Critical Political Biography

Dale T. McKinley

Pluto  Press

LONDON • CHICAGO, ILLINOIS

First published 1997 by Pluto Press
345 Archway Road, London N6 5AA
and 1436 West Randolph
Chicago, Illinois 60607, USA

British Library Cataloguing in Publication Data
A catalogue record for this book is available from the British Library

ISBN 0 7453 1282 9 hbk

Library of Congress Cataloging in Publication Data
A catalogue record for this book is available from the
Library of Congress

Designed and produced for Pluto Press by
Chase Production Services, Chadlington, OX7 3LN
Typeset from disk by Stanford DTP Services, Northampton
Printed in the EC by Redwood Books, Trowbridge

Contents

Acknowledgements

The long journey of this book would never have been as rewarding, or even possible, without good samaritans, comradely critics, loving partners and supportive friends and family. At the risk of selectivity, I must mention those who have been central. I would never have been able to complete the original dissertation without the tremendous assistance of Julius Nyang'goro and the endless enthusiasm and work of Debby Crowder and Dineane Buttram of the African and Afro-American Studies Department at the University of North Carolina-Chapel Hill. My long-time comrade-in-arms Keith Griffler, besides having my utmost respect for his towering intellect and revolutionary energy, contributed immensely to my understanding of classical Marxist theory. For their unflagging support and friendship through the years, my love and thanks go to Susan Blanchard, Lisa House, Joey Templeton, Marguerite Arnold, Jill Nystrom, Harry Trakoshis and Florencia Belvedere.

On the southern African side I greatly benefited from innumerable late-night debates with my comrade and housemate Langa Zita, heated arguments with Patrick Bond and from numerous discussions with my comrades in the South African Communist Party. The companionship and support of Sheila Wilson, Heidi Kriz, Pla Trakoshis, Bronwyn Nowitz and Dominique Lauyks helped me through many rough times. During my writing 'hibernation' in the Eastern Highlands of Zimbabwe, Richard and Fiona Eatwell kept me sane, and my thanks and respect go to Pat and Paul Brickhill who proved that revolutionaries can have families and still have fun.

As for all the usual stuff about my bearing sole responsibility for what I have written, I willingly accepted the challenge and am equally willing to accept the consequences. In this vein, comradely thanks must be given to Roger van Zwanenberg of Pluto Press for his commitment to publish this work, to Rachel Houghton for giving generously of her time, energy and editorial expertise and to the rest of the Pluto crew who made it possible.

Lastly, but in a way most central, is my family. To my sister Marsha a huge thanks for her willingness to listen and stand by a very troublesome brother, and to my other sister Margaret who will always remain a silent supporter. I cannot adequately express my love and respect for my parents Hugh and Becky McKinley who, while probably wishing that I had become a preacher of a different sort, instilled in me a qualitative sense of equality and justice which I hope has been true to those to whom it has been directed.

Dale Thomas McKinley
Johannesburg, 1997

Preface

The genesis of this book reflects much the same spirit as that contained in the liberation slogan, *a luta continua!* – the struggle goes on! Back in 1987/88 I found myself in war-torn El Salvador attending the birthday party of a leftist activist who was also a Jesuit priest. Despite the language barrier it became very clear that here was an ordinary man, who, in the face of daily death threats from the fascist military regime, continued to believe that it was possible for the ordinary mass of workers and poor to take revolutionary control of their own lives. It was the strength and conviction of that vision, for which the priest later paid with his life, which came to inform my own critical search to understand South Africa's liberation struggle.

After several years of weathering numerous assaults from conservative academia and erstwhile American 'democrats' during my studies in the US, I returned home to southern Africa, task in hand. Although I had spent the better part of my life in southern Africa, coming to live in South Africa in early 1991 was to be the start of a compelling experience. Through my work in running a political bookshop in Johannesburg, I began to develop strong links with those at the centre of the liberation struggle.

For the next two-and-a-half years I had a bird's eye view of South Africa's transition, combining occasional research with intense spells of activism. The experience of marching and dancing with tens of thousands of workers, being part of the seething masses at Chris Hani's funeral, organising critical debates among revolutionary theorists and activists, and being able to provide previously unavailable revolutionary literature made for interesting times. I couldn't have asked for a better way in which to ground the vision I had set out to engage critically.

Out of these experiences comes this book. It does not attempt to look objectively at the liberation struggle, but is work born of my desire to make a critical contribution to the ongoing struggle of the workers and the poor (not only South African), and to realise the vision of a socialist society in which material and mental creativity is no longer held hostage to narrow nationalism and the accumulative oppression of capitalism. While I have made substantive changes to my original dissertation in order to present a much clearer political argument, this book reflects the core of my observations, experiences and beliefs surrounding the struggle for South Africa's liberation.

Grounding the Critique

A luta continua! This popular slogan continues to resonate at least in one part of the world – South Africa. Three hundred years after the first European settlers arrived at the ironically named Cape of Good Hope in the 1600s, a struggle of liberation, varying in content and degree, has been waged within and outside its borders. It is a struggle that has followed the historical mutation of global mercantilism, modern capitalist development and penetration, and their uniquely South African by-products. Infused with a range of often peculiarly distinct racial, national and class conflicts, the struggle for liberation in South Africa has provided an enduring source of inspiration for many people the world over.

This book is about that struggle and one of the organisations that has now come to occupy centre stage, the African National Congress (ANC). The core of the book revolves around the strategy and tactics of the externalised (or exiled) ANC and its alliance partner, the South African Communist Party (SACP), focusing in particular on the last three decades. Because of the incredibly close relationship between the SACP and the ANC since 1950 (when the SACP was banned), it should be noted that I will not always distinguish between the two, but rather use the term ANC to encompass the SACP as well. Where there is a specific need to demarcate the policies and activities of the two, I will refer specifically to the SACP by name. The time-frame of this study ends in 1993 with the agreement for the installation of a Transitional Executive Council (TEC). This was the transitional institutionalised form of the negotiated political settlement forged between the ANC and the ruling (white) National Party (NP). The short-lived rule of the TEC and the subsequent victory of the ANC in the April 1994 elections signalled a qualitatively distinct era in the history of the South African struggle, which remains open for future analysis.

As much as South Africa's liberation struggle has, historically, provided a wellspring of inspiration to so many across the globe, there is a need to assess critically its historical character and direction. This study offers such a critique by analysing the dialectic between the fluid objective (structural) conditions within which the ANC (and the SACP) conducted their liberation struggle and the (subjective) choice of strategy and tactics the organisations (with special focus on leadership) pursued.

I argue that this dialectic has, despite appearances to the contrary, undermined the basis for any genuine realisation of the ANC's stated goal of struggle – national liberation for the transfer of power to the people. The inclusion of the period after the February 1990 unbanning of the ANC and its internal resuscitation will serve to show the most immediate results of such a dialectic.

National liberation has always been the declared goal of the ANC and its partner, the SACP. However, there have been many times when this alliance – especially after the incorporation of the Congress of South African Trade Unions (COSATU) in 1986 – has proposed the ultimate goal of socialism for South Africa. Although this goal is associated more with the SACP and COSATU than with the ANC itself, there has been such an overlap of membership that to disassociate the goal of socialism from the ANC is a misdirected and convenient omission. This is not to say that the ANC has ever had a coherent programme grounded in socialist ideology, but rather that large parts of the ANC's constituency have put forward a socialist vision. Whether or not this has filtered through to the ANC leadership and informed the strategy and tactics of the organisation is an entirely different matter.

As will be made clear, the ideological orientation of the ANC, as expressed through its leadership structures, has followed a pattern of what can be called 'incorporation'. This represents strategic ideological choices on the part of the ANC rather than an undulating (and self-propelled) tactical terrain. To put it another way, I shall argue that the ANC-led struggle for the liberation of South Africa has ignored the very people in whose name that struggle was conducted. Apart from the unique material and social character of the South African situation and the undoubted moral authority of the anti-apartheid struggle (both of which historically have contributed to a generally uncritical endorsement of the ANC), the bottom line is that the ANC has failed its mass constituency. By providing a critical historical analysis of the liberation struggle, this study serves to show the basis and outcome of such a failure.

And yet, this study attempts to go beyond an analytical interpretation of the facts. By revealing how the liberation movement has responded, both pro- and reactively, to the changing historical conditions under which its struggle has laboured, a much clearer picture emerges of the connection between choices and possibilities. Equally, such an approach reveals much about the ways in which revolutionary leadership interprets and acts upon both the structural conditions that contextualise the struggle they lead and the role of the agency which seeks to change those conditions.

Consequently the rich and varied activities of the rank and file are highlighted as integral to an understanding of actual and potential outcomes of struggle. In this way, analysis becomes more than just an intellectual exercise in methodological construction and application of theory – it can become a basis for future, critically informed intellectual investigation, as well as empowering for those to whom it is directed.

On a wider scale this study has relevance to situations beyond South Africa's borders. Although the ANC's struggle possesses its own distinct historical characteristics, most other liberation movements in the so-called third world also conducted (and some still conduct) their struggles in the name of national liberation for the people. Yet even a cursory analysis of the post-independence politics of (victorious) movements reveals the mutual problematic – the 'people' have consistently been ignored, if not oppressed, in new and inventive ways.

Any attempts to alter substantively the balance of forces in favour of the people will also have to deal with an international environment in which capitalism, and its free market politics, wreak havoc across the globe and in which the mass mobilisation necessary to effect genuinely transformative liberation no longer (centrally) revolves around the barrel of a gun.

Some Theoretical Considerations

The critical context of this work is grounded firmly within a classical Marxist-Leninist framework. For Marx, it was through an analysis of the contradictory relationship between the material productive forces of society and the consequent productive relationships that the key to understanding revolutionary 'epochs' was to be found. Thus,

> In considering such revolutions it is necessary always to distinguish between the material revolution in the economic conditions of production ... and the juridical, political, religious, aesthetic or philosophic – in a word, ideological forms wherein men become conscious of this conflict and fight it out. (Marx, 1970, pp. 20–1)

In other words, the specific form and character of such a revolution (revolutionary period) rest on the activities of those involved in the revolution (inclusive of all classes) within a particular, yet fluid, material context.

Although Marx and Lenin both located modern revolutionary change within the overall structure of capitalist relations, they constantly reiterated that the active and conscious involvement of those who were oppressed would ultimately determine the character and direction of change.[1] Neither Marx nor Lenin viewed revolution as following a structurally determined course, but rather located the 'self-activity', creativeness and 'outcome' of revolution precisely in the practice of those who make it – the oppressed. It is this recognition that allows a creative analysis of the conditions within which revolutionary activity takes place, encompassing both objective and subjective factors.

Marx and Lenin also applied the concept of social revolution (as the struggle to realise socialism) to the question of the struggle for national liberation. For them the two were inseparable. Thus Lenin argued,

> The ... revolution will be an era of a whole series of battles ... on all economic and political questions including national questions. It is the resolution of the sum of conflicts stemming from all these unresolved issues that will produce a social revolution ... all democratic demands [including] the self-determination of nations, must be rounded off and united in the demand for revolutionary struggle against capitalism. (Lenin, 1947, p. 64)

While this perspective incorporates both the differences and mutuality of national liberation and socialism, the central argument is that there can be no meaningful national liberation without a simultaneous struggle against what lies at the root of national oppression – capitalism and imperialism. In short, national liberation – influenced or driven by whatever demographic and/or culturally specific factors – can be little more than a political shift of the ruling class without a corresponding transformation in social relations; that is, without a class revolution.

Despite the repeated pronouncements of the death of Marxist-Leninist theory, its continued relevance is grounded in three simple, yet fundamental, reasons: first, the materialist basis of Marx's and Lenin's analyses, by pointing to the material foundations of all human interaction and conflict, remains central in our attempts to understand and analyse social processes; second, since different forms of capitalism continue to represent the dominant characteristic of national and global political economy (as they have for the past century), a critically informed Marxist-Leninist perspective allows a more holistic analysis and investigation of the social struggles that take place;[2] and last, as applied specifically to the history and post-liberation practice of national liberation movements, Marx's and Lenin's arguments concerning the political economy of imperialism and class have been borne out in practice.[3] This study explores the extent to which the relevance of such theoretical and strategic perspectives applies in the case of South Africa's national liberation struggle.

Casting a critical eye over the last decade, a strong case can be made that classical Marxist theories concerning capitalist society, social change and social conflict remain as relevant as ever. Despite recent events in the former USSR and Eastern Europe – events that many see as proof of the bankruptcy of Marxism – we have only to look critically at the recent past to reach a radically different conclusion.

While some things change, others simply become more transparent. As has been the case in South Africa for decades, the vast majority of humanity is either directly or indirectly suffering under a capitalist-dominated political economy. To the extent that there have existed, and continue to exist, variants of classic Western capitalist society, so too will the sustainability of these systems be dependent on basic freedoms and material benefit for the vast majority.

It would seem highly irrational to announce the timely 'death' of classical Marxism, specifically as it applies to revolution, when all around the world the reality is one of capitalism's ravages and the social conflict to which these give birth. Herein lies the durability and utility of classical Marxist theory: it links 'the causes and consequences of revolution directly to the historical emergence and transcendence of capitalism' (Skocpol and Trimberger, 1978, p. 122).

This does not mean that liberation struggles are helpless hostages to the dominant economic and political structure, just as they are not merely reducible to the activity of individuals. Rather, they are 'conditioned by changing structural economic conditions, state reforms and repression, international acts, imported ideas, leadership debates, and efforts to learn from mistakes' (A. Marx, 1992, p. 27). It is this combination of structure and struggle, set within the historical context of the ANC's liberation struggle, that informs this study.

There is also a rich body of literature that focuses on imperialism as central to any analysis of revolutionary activity and potential. Although this body of theory is by no means homogeneous in its approaches or prescriptions, recognition and analysis of imperialism are essential to a contemporary study of national liberation struggle.

With the continued transformation of global capitalism and endless conflicts around class, nation and race, it would be intellectually prudent to suspend any funeral arrangements for theories of imperialism. These theories provide a conceptual apparatus for exploring the process of transnationalisation of economic, political, ideological and military structures. By identifying the logic of power and analysing the activities of those with the capacity to exercise that power on a global scale, theories of imperialism have transcended time-specific application.

The Need for a Systematic Historical Critique

The literature on the history of the ANC's struggle, much like the more general theoretical works on revolution, offers limited analytical depth and application. While the academic historiographies cover, in some detail, the period up to the mid-1980s, the focal point of all these analyses is on the internal history of the ANC, the domestic conditions to which it responded and how these conditions informed the organisation's structure and programme. The limited time-frames do not allow for an analysis of the full historical panorama of ANC politics.

Studies carried out by ANC members and sympathisers follow the same general line. As might be expected, there is a general lack of both a critical political perspective and any serious theoretical grounding. It is indicative of the gap that exists between practical versus written contributions that these 'internal' studies represent the only available 'histories' of the ANC. The few studies that have focused on the external environment within which the ANC has operated do so from a very generalised (and often purely descriptive) perspective. As a result, these studies are useful for short-term insights but do not offer a systematic perspective of the ANC's externalised *cum* post-1990 struggle.

Although a great deal of heated debate has centred on the strategy and tactics of the ANC since its unbanning, very little has been published for widespread public consumption. What has found its way into the public arena has come from long-time critics of the ANC. While many internal ANC documents have been circulated for debate within the organisation, these have stayed within a fairly small circle of intellectuals and activists. As a result, the larger ANC membership, academics and activists, and the general public have only a vague idea about the extent and character of the debate on ANC strategy and subsequent policy. This book goes some way to fill the gap.

The Formative Years

> it is of less importance to us whether capitalism is smashed or
> not. It is of greater importance to us that while capitalism exists,
> we must fight and struggle to get our full share and benefit from
> the system.
>
> Dr Xuma, President-General of the ANC (1945)[1]

In order to provide the necessary historical background, this chapter
begins with a brief overview of colonial conquest (both English and
Afrikaner) and the introduction of capitalism in South Africa.
Within this historical context, the class character of the newly
formed ANC (founded in 1912) is linked directly to the parallel
development of an early politics of incorporation. In turn, it is argued
that this led to the ANC's historic preference for a programme of
ideological and class accommodation.

This early politics of incorporation was predominately responsible
for the defeat of any working-class-led socialist alternative to
nationalism during the 1920s and 1940s – the alternative potentially
coming from the Communist Party of South Africa (CPSA) and
the newly formed trade unions. What emerged was the institutionalisation of an analytically and practically circumscribed struggle
for national liberation. The rise of the decidedly narrow nationalism
of the ANC Youth League during the late 1940s (alongside that
of the victorious National Party) solidified what was to become a
defining trait of the ANC's struggle – the separation of national
liberation from material/social liberation. Finally, through an
analysis of the political content and form of ANC-led struggles
waged during the 1950s, it is argued that the ANC's strategy of
internal mass mobilisation failed on its own terms to alter radically
the political and socioeconomic status quo. In turn, this failure
created the conditions for a reactive turn to externalised struggle.

Setting the Scene of Struggle

After British control of the Cape colony was established in 1806
there began the oppression of ever-increasing numbers of indigenous
peoples. On the one hand, there were the independent-minded
'Afrikaners/Boers', who wanted to escape the limited economic

opportunities and 'liberal' racial policies imposed by the British colonial authorities in the Cape colony; and on the other, the rapacious appetite of an ever-expanding British imperialism/colonialism for the potential riches of the subcontinent.

As a result of their desire for more independence many of the Afrikaners who had been living in the Cape colony moved inland on what has come to be known as the 'Great Trek'. Unlike the subsequent Nationalist Party-inspired myth of the Trek as an all-conquering white 'army', the settlers made their way inland gradually through a combination of military setbacks and victories, as well as a great deal of trading and deal-making with local indigenous populations (Worden, 1994, pp. 11–18).

Throughout the nineteenth century wars of dispossession were waged against the kingdoms of the Xhosa, Tswana, Pedi, Sotho, Venda and Zulu (amongst others) by both the Afrikaners and the British. Parallel to these various wars were the continual conflicts and movements amongst the various indigenous peoples themselves. Starting with the *Mfecane* (Zulu for 'crushing') in 1818, when King Shaka embarked on an expansion of the Zulu 'state', profound social and geopolitical upheavals reverberated throughout the subcontinent. Many people were absorbed into the Zulu 'state', while others regrouped in new locations and re-established themselves as functioning kingdoms.

The combination of colonialist military and commercial advance and the ongoing rivalries and disputes within the indigenous population produced a uneven process of resistance and subjugation. Some people, such as the Pedi (situated along the Eastern Cape seaboard), were forcibly absorbed into the ranks of labourers as early as the 1840s to service the expanding colonialist commerical and military adventures; others, such as the Zulu and Sotho, managed to remain independent as kingdoms until the 1870s, containing the colonialist advance through a combination of astute economic and political cooperation and military prowess (Pampallis, 1991, pp. 3–13). Faced with vast disadvantages in military technology, cross-cultural unity and geographical dispersion, the majority of the indigenous peoples nevertheless offered stiff resistance to their inevitable defeat.

With the discovery of diamonds in the Kimberley area in 1867, followed by gold in the Witswatersrand in 1886, the South African colony was thrust headlong into a new era of capitalist accumulation. Within a few years much of the political, economic and social landscape had been transformed beyond recognition. Alongside a wave of new white immigration came a massive influx of machinery and capital goods necessary to exploit and process this vast accumulation of wealth. As could be expected, this capitalist invasion brought with it more efficient forms of oppression for the majority of the indigenous peoples, large sections of whom became wage workers on the mines or general labour for expanding capitalist enterprises.[2] The British colonial apparatus, urged on by international financiers and budding private/settler capital, launched an aggressive policy of increased political and administrative control over the South African hinterland in order to facilitate the control and use of African labour.

This process of capitalist expansion in South Africa is distinguishable from other African colonial conquests in that it created the largest, most concentrated and wealthiest white settler community and black working class on the continent (*circa* late 1800s). The creation of large cities around the mining compounds (the population of Kimberley, for example, went from virtually zero to tens of thousands in the space of 2–3 years) was the beginning of large-scale urbanisation of the indigenous population – something that was delayed in other African nations until well after colonial independence. It should also be noted that this capitalist expansion encompassed many beyond the borders of what was then the South African colony. Indigenous workers came from all over the subcontinent to work on the mines, providing the first link in what was to become an increasingly dependent economic relationship between South Africa and its neighbours. From 1874 until the end of the century, 'an estimated 10,000 African laborers were employed annually' in the diamond mines. Once the gold mines were in full production, the number of African workers employed between 1890 and 1899 'increased from 15,000 to an estimated 107,000' (Murray, 1982, pp. 128–30).

With this increased urbanisation and proletarianisation came the first opportunities for the nascent African working class, already administratively and physically separated from white workers, to organise. While there were some efforts to do so, the character of working-class 'industrial relations' consisted predominantly of ad hoc wage negotiations or moving from place to place in order to secure higher wages and better conditions. But even these efforts came increasingly under attack from the demands of competing and expanding mining companies on the colonial administration to ensure an abundant and compliant workforce (Jeeves, 1982, pp. 137–81).

Not surprisingly the British imperialists wanted sole control of South Africa which was now seen as a prize colonial possession. This clashed with the Afrikaner vision of an independent African empire of their own. Mutual greed led to what has come to be called the Boer Wars (1899–1902). After intense fighting and the use of brutal methods of control (for example, the use of concentration camps to detain the Afrikaners), the British eventually prevailed. In the process, however, they created an Afrikaner community whose messianic vision of rightful control of the land and its inhabitants would lead eventually to their political ascendancy. In the midst of the intra-colonialist feuds over the spoils of capitalist exploitation the vast majority of indigenous peoples played the (unwilling) role of economic pawns, creating wealth over which they had no control.

Soon after the signing of the Vereeniging peace treaty in 1902 between the British and the Afrikaners – which set the stage for the eventual 'independence' of South Africa from Britain – a new round of accumulation and exploitation resumed. This necessitated even greater political and economic control over the population, as well as a vast pool of cheap labour needed to underpin the ever-expanding mining and industrial base. Mining companies and newly formed manufacturing industries began to make vociferous demands on the colonial administration to adopt stricter measures to control African labour; but it was the mining sector in particular which wanted to find new ways of securing cheaper labour in order to enhance their competitiveness and reap super-profits with the added benefit of an internationally fixed gold price. Parallel to this was the influx of rural Afrikaners to the larger cities in search of work, where they increasingly demanded further extensions of racially based social privilege and special work protection. This, combined with the specific material needs of colonial capitalism, resulted in a concerted assault on even those limited political and economic rights that Africans had managed to retain (for example, freehold land title, limited voting rights in the Cape colony and limited freedom of movement in urban areas).

The next few years saw a series of new laws designed to meet the political and economic interests of the white population and an ever-expanding capitalism. The draft South Africa Act, published in February 1909, was the opening shot in this battle to institutionalise racialised social engineering. The Act, the main purpose of which was to unite the Afrikaner and British communities, ensured that virtually all political and economic power would be vested in white hands and thus gave the new parliament the ability to institute wide-ranging measures in order to facilitate control over all aspects of African life. The draft Act was formally adopted by the newly constituted all-white South African parliament on 31 May 1910 as the Act of Union.

This Act was followed by a series of racially based Acts during the period 1911–13. These included: the Dutch Reformed Church Act, which excluded blacks from membership of the church; the Mines and Works Act for the protection of white workers; the Immigrants Restriction Act to keep 'undesirables' out of the country; the Native Labour Regulation Act to control black labourers; and the Defence Act which established the basis for a white- dominated defence force. This was in addition to the already existing 'pass system', which had been introduced in 1896 as a means to control the movement and employment of the black population; and a discriminatory poll tax.

While all this legislation imposed further enslavement and humiliation on the African population, it was the measures implemented in the lead-up to the passage of the Native Land Act of 1913 which finally proved to be the spur to the formation of the first national organisation devoted to opposing the white-created racial order – the African National Congress (ANC; initially called the South African Native National Congress).

The main reasons for the passage of the Land Act were threefold: first, the desire of the expanding industrial and mining sector to take away land rights for Africans so they would be 'available' as cheap wage labour to facilitate capital accumulation; second, to impose on Africans unsustainable living and economic conditions by demarcating small and marginal 'Native Reserves' as living and productive space, leaving migrant labour as the only option for survival; and third, the growing opposition of white commercial farming interests and rural Afrikaner farmers (which included many who had lost their land and livelihood during the wars) to the presence of African squatters, sharecroppers and landowners who were 'competing' for land and, of course, material benefit (Bundy, 1982, pp. 228–30).

Opposition from white farming interests was due to the fact that a growing number of African land-owners were producing food more cheaply than most white farmers. Additionally, there were burgeoning business opportunities for other African rural dwellers (for example, transport) which took much business away from the predominantly Afrikaner rural white population. This rural African petty bourgeoisie were able to compete effectively on the 'market' due to social and family networks which often allowed for efficient use of labour power (Wilson, 1971, pp. 104–71). Further, continued growth and economic empowerment of an African petty bourgeoisie engendered a sociopolitical outlook which identified more closely with British 'civilisation', and an emergent 'free market' capitalism which gave space to petite-bourgeois accumulation. In short, there was every reason for industrial capital, Afrikaner politicians and white farmers to smash (or at least suppress) this new class.

The Land Act not only satisfied the accumulative demands of the capitalists and white farmers, but it also ended effectively the growth of what had been an expanding and relatively successful class of small African commercial farmers. The Act, which made it illegal for Africans to purchase or lease land outside the newly designated 'Native Reserves' (which comprised only 13 per cent of all land in the country), was attempting to close the principal avenue of petit-bourgeois class formation available to Africans (Bundy, 1982, p. 228). It was from this class that the leadership of the ANC were to come.

The Early ANC

During this time there had been various regional and localised attempts at organisation (for example, the Natal and Transvaal Native Congresses) and protests over lack of economic and political opportunities which were fast eroding under the racialised legislative onslaught. The formation of the ANC on 8 January 1912 in Bloemfontein represented the first serious attempt to establish a national forum to address the political and economic situation of the black population. As has been widely chronicled (Walshe, 1971; Meli, 1988; Mbeki, 1992), the majority of the members, and certainly the ANC leadership, were drawn mainly from the newly emergent black petty bourgeoisie as well as the traditional chiefs, whose interests were tied to the availability and use of land by Africans. This black petty bourgeoisie wanted to find ways to stem the assault on their own class interests (and movement), as well as on what they perceived as the general political and economic well-being of Africans.

To this endeavour the majority of the new ANC leaders brought with them not only their particular class politics but also the strong influence of a Christian education and its corresponding social mores. Thus a perspective emerged that incorporated a politics of non-violence and of incorporation; the main priority becoming one of persuading the 'civilised' British that the educated, propertied and 'civilised' Africans could be incorporated into the mainstream of South African society. The ANC leaders saw the limited Cape franchise, in which Africans qualified for the right to vote or to be elected on the basis of their wealth, as their goal. As one scholar has argued, the formation of the ANC was

> a reactive act, attributable to disappointment and anger with the white government's failure to deal 'responsibly' with its African subjects. Its mode was to re-act and object to unfavorable government acts using constitutional channels. (Dorabji, 1983, p. 34)

This has led some to dismiss the early ANC as nothing more than a 'bowl in hand' organisation which did nothing to challenge the status quo. While there has been a tendency to overstate the 'radical' potential of the early ANC, its contribution to a nascent sense of national consciousness should not be ignored. This is best exemplified by the following appeal from one of the ANC's leaders, P.I. Seme:

The demon of racialism, the aberrations of the Xhosa-Fingo feud, the animosity that exists between the Zulus and Tongaas, between the Basutos and every other Native must be buried and forgotten; it has shed among us sufficient blood! We are one people. These divisions, these jealousies, are the cause of all our woes and of all our backwardness and ignorance today. ('Imvo Zabantsundu', in Karis and Carter, 1972, p. 72)

However, the politics of the early ANC was far from radical. All their early political efforts centred on attempts to persuade both the British and South African governments to provide relief by constitutional means. When it became clear to the ANC leadership that the South African government was not receptive to their pleas, they dispatched deputations and delegations to London in the vain hope that the colonial power would side with the 'Africans' in their grievances. The ANC leaders pleaded for the application of what they perceived as the British sense of 'fair play and justice', which the 'Africans as loyal British subjects', would greatly appreciate (Meli, 1988, p. 47).

Despite the lack of positive responses from the British, the politics of deputation continued. However, after one such deputation to London in 1919, it finally became clear that the British were not going to intervene. Having no strategies other than those they had now exhausted, and without having gained a single concession, the ANC literally began to fall apart. As Peter Walshe has noted,

the support of the chiefs ebbed away, membership stagnated and later declined, and Congress began a long struggle through a quarter of a century of political frustration and organizational weakness that at times all but overwhelmed it. (Walshe, 1971, p.65)

In the years following the First World War, South African industry grew at a rapid pace, as did the workforce. 'Between 1915–1916 and 1919–1920, the numbers of factories rose from 3998 to 6890 and factory employment by 73%' (Kaplan, 1982, p. 303). One by-product of this was the further proletarianisation of the African labour force. There was also the formation of organisations which, to varying degrees, represented sections of this growing working class (both white and black): the International Socialist League (ISL); the first African union under the name Industrial Workers of Africa (IWA); the Industrial and Commercial Workers Union (ICU); and in 1921 the Communist Party of South Africa (CPSA).

This expanding, but still fairly politically inactive, working class staged several strikes, the largest of which was the 1920 mineworkers' strike, and intermittent campaigns against discriminatory laws (for example, the anti-pass law campaign by women in the Orange Free State province). And yet it played a minor role within the ANC, whose leadership rejected organising amongst the mass of Africans. There was also some organisation among the white working class. White workers belonging to the newly formed CPSA embarked on strikes and agitated for a new government based on the Soviet model. However, some of these early 'communists' were no less racist than those they wanted to replace, and marched under banners proclaiming: 'Workers Unite for a White South Africa'. Meanwhile, the system of racial discrimination was further entrenched as racial capitalism delivered the goods with perverted efficiency. (It should be noted that the term 'racial capitalism' has found widespread use among many South African analysts and activists to describe the peculiarly South African version of exploitation and accumulation practised by white minority capital and government. Even though formal apartheid was not instituted until after the election victory of the all-white National Party in 1948, most of the elements of a racially defined labour and social system designed to service the needs of capitalist accumulation were well entrenched long before.)

'Front' Politics and Lost Opportunities

By the mid-1930s the ANC was a terribly weak organisation. In large part this can be attributed to the continued erosion of its active social base, which was directly linked to the effects of government legislation such as the Land Act. In addition, the unfavourable economic conditions of the Depression era further dented the material and organisational well-being of ANC members and sympathisers, most of whom came from the African petty bourgeoisie.

Another important reason for the decline of the ANC was the way in which the leadership responded and reacted to increased political and economic oppression instituted by the white minority government. The continued and dominant strategy of attempting to persuade and court the white elite (both internal and external) proved both futile and disempowering. This outcome was linked directly to the general failure of the ANC to organise proactively beyond its dominant petit-bourgeois base, weakening any links it did have with the mass of Africans. Many of the ministers, urban intellectuals, traditional chiefs, landowners and small entrepreneurs who had formed the organisational core of the ANC had turned to more narrow professional and business pursuits. Others were absorbed into the state administration as the government sought to expand its civil service alongside its extended control of every aspect of African life. As far as the ANC's social support base – the independent African peasantry – was concerned, the cumulative effects of the Land Act and worsening economic conditions had forced many back into a 'survival mode' of wage labour, which limited their ability to engage in organised political activity. The main question that came to be asked by many ANC veterans was what, if any, attempts should be made to revitalise the organisation. Some leaders, like the CPSA's J.B. Marks, were already pronouncing the ANC 'literally dead' (Fine and Davis, 1990, p. 99).

The active–dormant stages that the ANC went through during the early 1900s were to foreshadow a similar pattern throughout the history of its struggle. What this initial period reflected was the dialectic of struggle set out in the Introduction, a dialectic that encompassed a combination of changing structural conditions and the general strategic and organisational response from the ANC's leadership. As long as there was some sort of immediate crisis or new law to be opposed the ANC responded with varying degrees of activity and resistance. However, once their responses had either been suppressed, undermined by cooption or had failed on their own terms, the ANC lapsed into a state of near-paralysis until the next round of favourable circumstances was presented.

This is not to say that the ANC did nothing in between (for example, deputations, delivering petitions, organising meetings), but rather that its reluctance and/or perceived inability to set about the task of long- term grassroots organising among the masses of South Africans became the hallmark of ANC strategy and tactics. Lack of grassroots organising can be traced to two main factors. First, the dominant petit-bourgeois class interests of the ANC leadership (selective land ownership, access to capital, a 'free market'), to be secured by limited participation in a bourgeois parliament, did not lend themselves to close identification with the interests of the workers and unemployed. Second, the conscious strategy of adopting a politics of accommodation bound the interests of the ANC much more closely to those classes who held the reins of (or had greater access to) political and economic power. As we shall see, this has had its own particular logic and effects on the possibilities and potential for realising any genuine national liberation in general, and for radical transformation in particular.

Given the parlous state of the ANC as an effective political organisation, the general sullen character of the liberation struggle and the confidence with which the white government was acting, there was a desperate need for new initiatives and political direction. Added to these problems, the period 1935–36 saw the newly elected government of Prime Minister Hertzog introduce further discriminatory legislation which finally abolished the limited Cape franchise, entrenched the 1913 Land Act to prevent Africans from any further purchase of land, and created a separate 'Native Representative Council' controlled by the white government. It was these increasingly oppressive political and economic measures that spurred the ANC to participate in the convening of the All Africa Convention (AAC) at the end of 1935.

Participation in the AAC, which brought together for the first time Coloureds, Black Nationalists, Communists and Trotskyists, was a marked departure from previous ANC practice, which had generally confined itself to a narrow, blacks-only policy. One of the more significant results of this opening up was to put the ANC, for the first time, in at least indirect alliance with the Communist Party of South Africa (CPSA) – a relationship that was to prove increasingly important for, and influential on, the ANC.

The AAC was the first real attempt to bring together a wide range of anti-racist organisations and individuals in some sort of loose alliance in order to resist the ever more restrictive and oppressive ravages of racial capitalism. In many ways this represented an organisational step forward in the struggle against white capital and government. However, this was only in so far as the resultant strategy and tactics also moved forward from what had already been attempted (and failed): to mobilise direct challenges to the system. Unfortunately, it soon became clear that the leading elements in the AAC (predominantly from the ANC) were not seriously interested in any substantive and forceful rethinking of strategy and tactics, but rather, wanted more people to carry out the same activities as before. In short, the AAC remained wedded to the stale strategy of deputations and faith in superior moral arguments.

It was during these debates over tactics that there began to emerge within the ANC a younger generation of African intellectuals and professionals who wanted to go beyond what they perceived as an outdated politics of deputation and (Anglo-inspired) liberalism. This nascent bloc within the ANC, which gathered pace throughout the late 1930s and 1940s, was later to find expression in the ANC Youth League (ANCYL). At this stage though, they remained in the background. While there were those in the AAC – mostly the Trotskyites – who pushed for a more direct approach to action (for example, boycotting the newly formed Native Representative Council), the end result was a politics of ideological and class accommodation.

Such a politics, albeit pursued at a particularly youthful stage in the development of the liberation struggle, was to become the hallmark of the ANC and its future alliance partners. This can partly be explained by what has turned out to be an ageless tradition within the ANC alliance and particularly in its leadership: holding the firm belief that accommodating the widest possible spectrum of ideological and class interests, and attempting to suppress differences between such interests, will present the surest and shortest route to national liberation.

It was during the years 1936–45 that the logic of this kind of liberation politics became the guiding principle of the ANC and in particular its alliance partner the CPSA. For its part, the CPSA had followed dutifully the dictates of Moscow by pursuing the strategy of a 'people's front'. In theory, the 'people's front' strategy stressed the need to bring together all social forces that might play a positive role in furthering the demands of national liberation. In practice it meant two things: first, marginalising the black working class as a major force for radical change in favour of 'progressive' white labour, 'liberal' British/international capital and a decidely narrow black African nationalism; and second, identifying socialism (that is, working-class politics) as a mostly foreign (white) ideology which was not appropriate to 'African conditions' and thus an obstacle to the national liberation of the black majority of South Africa. Although many observers have blamed the failed strategy of accommodation wholly on African nationalism, it was the CPSA's influential strategic outlook that should bear at least equal blame.

While the CPSA was following the 'people's front' strategy as an obedient member of the Stalinist-dominated Third International (Communist), the core of the ANC leadership would no doubt have seen the strategy as fitting with their own vision of a (predominantly) elite-led national liberation movement. Such a vision (encapsulated in Xuma's quote, which forms the epigraph to this chapter) would thus be more likely to prioritise links and tactical alliances with 'liberal' capital and the black petty bourgeoisie, rather than consistently and firmly prioritise the leading role of the black working class.

Controlled by a moderate leadership unable to transcend its own limited vision, the ANC found common ground with the CPSA in their 'people's front' strategy. Throughout the early 1940s this strategy led to support for the allied war effort and the active discouragement of militant mass action.[3] Exemplifying the ANC leadership's approach was a letter from Dr Xuma (President-General of the ANC) to General Smuts (co-leader in the South African government) in 1942 which stated:

> We are alarmed at the number of avoidable strikes that have taken place recently ... We deplore the occurrence of any strike at the present time, as we realise that they tend to impede the national war effort as well as to strain race relations between blacks and whites ... We are anxious not to embarrass the government ... We humbly and respectfully request the Prime Minister to receive a deputation from the ANC and CNETU

(Council of Non-European Trade Unions) ... to assist you toward settlement of recent strikes and prevention of future strikes. (Xuma Papers, in Fine and Davis, 1990, pp. 46–7)

Despite the dominant ANC strategy of limiting mass action, the years following the end of the Second World War saw extensive strikes by the black working class, the most notable being the 1946 mineworkers' strike on the Witswatersrand in which an estimated 50,000–100,000 workers took part. The strike was put down violently by the state, followed by the arrest of almost the entire Central Committee of the CPSA, who were charged with instigating an illegal strike. This happened at a time when the white, predominantly English-speaking ruling class was seeking some sort of solution to both the potentially disruptive power of labour and the rise of Afrikaner political aspirations. Above all, the interests of white capital had to be protected and the 'cooperation' of black labour secured.

In practice what such cooperation meant was the realisation by this sector of the white ruling class that their very existence and wealth depended on finding ways to control and coopt the black working class (and/or its leadership). This dilemma was to underlie the creation of the apartheid system, the eventual crisis of apartheid and the realisation of its limitations, as well as moves to find new ways of securing capitalist interests in different forms.

Since the general programme of the ANC posed little threat to the interests of the white ruling class, it was the black labour movement that bore the brunt of state repression. While the eventual defeat of the labour movement during the 1940s was linked predominantly to the accommodative and disempowering politics of the ANC (alongside the CPSA), there were other contributory factors: first, the class structure of South African society ensured that the 'social weight of the proletariat as a force for democratic change' was still weak, although the political strategy of the ANC only contributed to such general weakness; and second, the 'weakness of liberalism as a political force within the ruling class and the decisiveness with which the ruling class as a whole attacked the organised labour movement' made working-class struggles that much more difficult (Fine and Davis, 1990, p. 99).

By the end of the decade the South African liberation landscape looked decidedly barren. The black working-class and labour movements were reeling under the defeats they had suffered, the 'people's front' of the ANC and CPSA remained stuck in an outmoded and failed politics of accommodation, and the right-wing Afrikaner-controlled National Party – promising even harsher suppression of the black population – had gained control of the country in the 1948 white elections.

What emerged from this period was the decisive defeat of a working-class-led socialist alternative to African nationalism in the struggle for South African liberation. Much of the impetus for this development lies on the doorstep of the CPSA and its policy of submerging independent working-class organisation and interests under the banner of a broad-based alliance with African nationalism as its guiding principle.

While the CPSA was not solely responsible for this development, it was the CPSA which chose to integrate itself so closely with the ANC and thus to identify with the decidedly petit-bourgeois character and politics of that movement. The strategic entry-point of the CPSA to the working class, and the working class's subsequent contact with the CPSA brand of socialism, was both limiting and deradicalising. Thus, from the start, not only did this strategy fundamentally weaken the black labour movement (and thus the African masses as a whole), but it created the conditions in which socialism was viewed as inappropriate and/or an obstacle to the immediate liberation struggle. National liberation was thus analytically and practically circumscribed. Put another way, the national liberation struggle became detached from the concomitant struggle for social and material liberation of the South African masses. As a result, African nationalism became politically and strategically hegemonic, albeit in a slightly more radicalised form. From this point, the ANC was to be the major vehicle for that new hegemony.

Dual Nationalisms

By the end of 1949 there were two new organisations that reigned supreme among their respective constituencies – the Afrikaner-dominated National Party and the ANC, now dominated by its Youth League. The respective hegemony of these two organisations gave rise to an ever-heightening duel of nationalist vision in which the respective nationalisms fed off each other, fuelling a parallel growth of Afrikaner and African nationalism which most observers have tended to ignore. As one analyst of nationalism has argued, 'nationalism is a parasitic movement and ideology shaped by what it opposes' (Breuilly, in Fine and Davis, 1990, p. 75).

After securing a narrow victory in the 1948 all-white elections, Prime Minister Daniel Malan and his National Party quickly set about the task of instituting a raft of laws and decrees that would entrench existing legalised racism and form the foundation for the specifically Afrikaner version of apartheid. The impetus to this development came from two sources: the need of the new National Party to secure the support of those sectors of white society (white working class, Afrikaner farmers, Afrikaner petite-bourgeoisie) who were threatened by industrialisation and further capitalist development; and the need to meet the new demands of such economic development (that is, increased exploitation of the black labour force). Although the historical development of apartheid has always had as much to do with class considerations as those of race, the racism of the National Party and racial history of South Africa provided a firm foundation on which to construct apartheid.[4]

In the space of less than two years the new government had introduced the Prohibition of Mixed Marriages Act, the Immorality Act (prohibiting inter-racial sexual relations), the Population Registration Act (a national roll according to racial classification), the Group Areas Act (demarcating all land use according to race) and the Suppression of Communism Act (outlawing the CPSA and giving wide powers to silence any person and/or organisation seeking change).

At the same time, the National Party embarked on a programme to ensure that Afrikaners would be given special economic privileges and security. The NP also nationalised key industries, putting them in the hands of the Afrikaner state and giving the nascent ruling class a powerful tool of accumulation and economic power. Although the NP had verbally assaulted the power and privilege of English-speaking capital, there soon emerged a quiet understanding that both stood to benefit from the 'new' apartheid programme. This understanding spread to international capital as well, which was always on the lookout for low-wage 'stable' environments in which to invest – especially when they knew their respective governments would support their business activities as anti-communist patriotism.[5]

Symptomatic of the supportive role played by international capital were the multi-million dollar loans extended to the National Party government during the 1950s by the World Bank, which had been set up by the victorious Western allies in 1945. After visiting South Africa on a fact-finding mission in 1950, the World Bank's vice-president, Robert Garner, reported that:

> The Bank's mission to South Africa is satisfied that the loan would be perfectly sound, and highly desirable for the bank to make, since South Africa's development is regarded as highly important. The mission found South Africa a fine, strong country of fine people and the loan would be an excellent banking proposition. The mission has been impressed by the variety of South Africa's industrial development ... credit standing ... and other sources of capital. (Legassick and Hemson, 1976)

Such perspectives set the tone for what was to become large-scale involvement of international finance capital in the South African economy. The increasing integration of the South African economy into the global capitalist system would provide an important source of economic support for the apartheid state and a source of profit for international capital. However, as the discussion in chapter 6 will show, South Africa's integration into the global capitalist economy would later prove a strategic godsend for an ANC struggle bereft of internal organisation and 'success'.

The Rise of the ANC Youth League

Against the backdrop of the 1940s and with increasing internal political and economic suppression of the black population, combined with a resurgent international anti-communist imperialism, the ANC Youth League found fertile ground for its ideological and organisational coup d'état. What the Youth League sought was a turn to more direct forms of mass-oriented struggle around a rejuvenated and 'pure' African nationalist movement. They viewed previous ANC failures as the result of the adoption of liberal and socialist ideas which were out of keeping with their own idealised vision of an African nationalism which would reclaim a sense of African community and clearly identify the enemy as the colonial/imperialist invader. The programme of the Youth League 'was not designed to push the ... programme of the African nationalist establishment beyond its liberal limits but rather to recapture the past in the name of an imagined community of Africans' (Fine and Davis, 1990, p. 74).

The Youth League set out a new vision for the ANC and African nationalism in its 1944 manifesto. Its 'Statement of Policy' read:

> The African, on his side, regards the Universe as one composite whole; an organic entity, progressively driving towards greater harmony and unity whose individual parts exist merely as interdependent aspects of one whole realising their fullest life in the corporate life where communal contentment is the absolute measure of values. His philosophy of life strives towards unity and aggregation; towards greater social responsibility.

Under the sub-heading 'Our Creed', the document stated:

- We believe in the divine destiny of nations.
- The goal of all our struggles is Africanism and our motto is *Africa's Cause Must Triumph*.
- We believe that the national liberation of Africans will be achieved by Africans themselves. We reject foreign leadership of Africa.

- We may borrow useful ideologies from foreign ideologies, but we reject the wholesale importation of foreign ideologies into Africa.
- We combat moral disintegration among Africans by maintaining and upholding high ethical standards ourselves.
- We believe in the unity of all Africans from the Mediterranean Sea in the North to the Indian and Atlantic oceans in the South – and that Africans must speak with one voice. (ANC Youth League Manifesto, in Mandela, 1990, pp. 12–19; emphasis in original)

Conjuring up images of an indivisible and inalienable African nationalism, the Youth League made its move at the ANC's annual conference in December 1949. Out went much of the old leadership and in came the Young Turks with their Programme of Action as the new beacon of the ANC. The one exception was the election of Dr James S. Moroka to the presidency (after Z.K. Matthews had declined the first nomination). Dr Moroka was one of the wealthiest African landowners in the country and certainly did not qualify as 'new blood'. Moroka was later to reveal just how much of a 'moderate' he was when he refused to endorse fully the mass actions of the organisation and distanced himself publicly from those actions in his trial for civil disobedience. However, many of the main posts went to Youth Leaguers including Nelson Mandela, Walter Sisulu and Oliver Tambo, although there was some continuity with the old leadership through men like Chief Albert Luthuli and Z.K. Matthews and CPSA members such as Moses Kotane and David Bopape.

The Programme of Action outlined what the demands of the ANC should be with the emphasis on seeking 'national freedom' and 'self-determination'. However, in terms of the political content of such demands the programme remained firmly within the liberal democratic tradition. It called for 'the right of direct representation in all the governing bodies of the country' and 'the abolition of all differential institutions or bodies specially created for Africans'.

The most important break with the old strategy and tactics, though, was the commitment to certain forms of direct action and mass mobilisation. The programme called for the employment of the following tactics: 'immediate and active boycott, strike, civil disobedience, non-cooperation and such other means' to accomplish their demands (Mandela, 1990, p. 29). Underlying the programme was the expectation that the masses would naturally respond to these calls. In this expectation the League was not altogether wrong.

Although the black working class and peasantry had been hard hit by the defeats of the 1940s and were reeling under the weight of the 'new' apartheid order, there remained an undying fighting spirit that was ready to be tapped. However, in its Programme of Action the League gave little emphasis to organising the working class or peasantry other than including a general call for a new workers' organisation to 'improve their standard of living', and an exhortation to 'develop' the African reserves and establish enterprises for 'employment' (Mandela, 1990, p. 29). None the less, the League's vision and strategy for a radicalised African nationalism, given the lack of any substantive programmatic challenges, partly filled the gap.

Despite the stated hostility of many Youth Leaguers to the role of the CPSA it was not long before its members began to reclaim influence and position within the ANC. This stemmed from two separate but equally important developments: the self-dissolution of the CPSA in 1950 (just after the passage of the Suppression of Communism Act) and its reconstitution in secret, although the ANC now became the main vehicle through which the CPSA worked (many white party members also joined the newly formed all-white Congress of Democrats – COD); and the adoption by the CPSA of an ideological framework in which it argued for the strategic primacy of what it termed 'revolutionary nationalism' over socialism.

The CPSA made the argument that 'black' South Africa was a 'colony' of its white oppressors. Calling for a 'revolutionary party of workers, peasants, intellectuals, and petty bourgeoisie' whose objective would be national liberation, the CPSA gave analytical and organisational content to what was to become known as the two-stage theory of struggle (SACP, 1981, pp. 200–11):

> This distinction [between a socialist movement struggling for socialism and a revolutionary nationalist movement struggling for national liberation] was vital for the forms of organisation and activity which the party was to support, its effect being to divide artificially the democratic and socialist aspects of the struggle into two separate compartments. (Fine and Davis, 1990, p. 113)

What this meant in practice was the subordination of explicit class struggle and organisation to the primary task of building a broad nationalist coalition of social forces to achieve the primary objective of national liberation.

Setting the Boundaries of Liberation

Other than the 1950 May Day stay-aways, which brought to light the untapped militancy of the black working class, as well as the harsh counter-measures white business and the state were willing to implement, little mass action or struggle took place until 1952.

In that year the ANC embarked on a national defiance campaign which was designed to repeal numerous government Acts passed since 1948 by bringing together, at national level, various local grievances that emanated from disparate communities. Although the defiance campaign has usually been described as an important turning point towards mass action and confirmation of the ANC's radicalisation, this is too simple an understanding.[6] Indeed, the way in which the campaign's strategy was determined and conducted raises serious questions about such an interpretation.

Conceived as a non-violent mass action campaign to put pressure on the ruling class for reforms, the defiance campaign followed the same strategic logic as previous efforts, that is, the belief that through moral argument and example the ANC could persuade the government to reform. Despite the stated need to bring together the mass of people in action, the core of the campaign centred on the example of the national leadership, which volunteered to engage in non-violent civil disobedience.

Little effort was made to organise the black urban working class, who were by far the most 'organisable' section of the masses owing to their concentration in urban areas and their general social conditions. But this was the character of the campaign, the main feature of which was to court arrest through highly public acts of civil disobedience –something that most workers could not afford to participate in for obvious reasons. One of the distinguishing features of the campaign was the grassroots involvement of women who protested vigorously at the proposed extension of the pass laws to them. This was an important development because women, who had been consciously left in the background of the liberation struggle by the ANC leadership, were just as consciously placing themselves and their own struggles on a liberation agenda dominated by patriarchal influences and practice.

Believing that a cautious, top-down, non-violent approach was the best, and only, way to conduct mass struggle, the ANC leadership turned a potentially useful tactic into a strategic principle. Fearing the power of the apartheid state, arguing that the masses were not prepared for militant confrontation and still believing in moral suasion, the ANC recoiled from mass mobilisation. The campaign achieved none of the reforms it had demanded.

While there is nothing wrong nor inherently deradicalising in principle about the tactical use of non-violent struggle, it was the strategic approach and conduct of the campaign that ensured that other forms of struggle engaged in by militant sections of the oppressed were either disregarded or actively suppressed. There were instances, particularly in the militant Eastern Cape region and in response to the victimisation of campaign participants, when workers embarked on wildcat strikes or called for indefinite general strikes with the support of the local ANC leadership. But in the case of the call for an indefinite general strike the ANC national leadership intervened and replaced it with a one-day protest strike (*Drum*, October 1952).

An argument can be made that the ANC leadership followed this strategic path for a number of reasons:

- fear that militant action would be premature and unorganised;
- belief that a more explicit challenge to the state would bring an extremely harsh response from the state which would potentially decapitate the movement;
- understanding that the international situation was particularly hostile to more militant activity by a 'third world' liberation movement.

While each of these reasons can be seen as a 'rational' choice/response to unfavourable existing conditions, the reality is that the strategic choices made were the result of the way in which the ANC leadership 'rationally' forged its ideological and strategic approach to mass struggle over a period of time. The possibilities of struggle present in the late 1950s (that is, combining objective conditions and subjective purpose) rested precisely on the degree to which the leadership of the dominant political movement, the ANC, interacted with and led the basic (materially located) struggles raised from the ground. Indeed, the character of that process related directly to the potentialities for change under fluid objective conditions. The leadership's decision to interpret those objective conditions as being static disempowered the rich potential of a struggle that had every possibility of equally altering the objective 'reality'.

In 1953 the logic of the ANC's nationalist programme resulted in the establishment of what came to be known as the Congress Alliance. The four distinct national groups (Black, White, Coloured, Indian) were represented in the Alliance by the ANC, the Congress of Democrats, the South African Coloured Organisation and the South African Indian Congress respectively. Included in the Alliance also were the newly formed South African Congress of Trade Unions (SACTU) and the predominantly white Federation of South African Women (FSAW). The irony was that the Alliance mirrored the racial categories of the apartheid state. National identification had come full circle.

Although the majority of the ANC leadership – there seemed to be little canvassing of the general membership's opinions – were clearly supportive of the formation of the Alliance, opposition was voiced. Arguing that the Alliance's liberal 'multiracialism' was undermining radical African nationalism, ANC Youth League members like Potlako Leballo and Robert Sobukwe opposed the

.ANC's participation in the Alliance. It was these men who were later to lead a splinter group out of the ANC and form the rival Pan Africanist Congress (PAC). There was also opposition from left critics of the ANC who, in the main, rejected the racial departmentalisation of the liberation movement. Much of the left critique, though, was unfortunately sectarian. Organisations like the Non-European Unity Movement (NEUM) derided and chastised the ANC for what they saw as 'collaborationist' politics and lack of a class outlook. However true these criticisms might have been, the NEUM in particular devolved into a fetishism of 'non-collaboration' while simultaneously organising itself as no more than a different version of collective nationalisms with little effort given to organising for the only real alternative to accommodationist nationalism: an independent working-class movement.

The first move of the Alliance was the decision to draw up the now famous Freedom Charter setting out its basic programme and demands. Conceptualised as a document that would express the views of the 'people' of South Africa, the Freedom Charter was to become the guiding manifesto of the ANC Alliance and would eventually be regarded by large numbers of the oppressed as representative of their aspirations. Drafted by a sub-committee of the National Action Committee, a body set up by the Alliance for this specific task, the Charter has often been presented by the ANC as representative of the 'voice' of the people of South Africa. Despite the impressive number of people who participated in the Charter's adoption at Kliptown in June 1955, the process by which the document was drawn up and adopted involved a select Alliance membership.[7]

Stating that South Africa 'belongs to all who live in it' and calling for 'a democratic state, based on the will of the people' the Charter set out a list of demands. These were grouped under the following headings:

- the people shall govern;
- all national groups shall have equal rights;
- the people shall share in the country's wealth;
- the land shall be shared among those who work it;
- all shall be equal before the law;
- all shall enjoy equal human rights;
- there shall be work and security;
- the doors of learning and culture shall be opened;
- there shall be houses, security and comfort;
- there shall be peace and friendship.

The underlying purpose behind each of these demands was a response to what ANC President Albert Luthuli called 'the conditions that obtain: harsh, oppressive, and unjust conditions'

(Luthuli, 1978). Indeed, the Charter came at a time when the apartheid government was consolidating its discriminatory legislation and conducting an increasingly concerted assault on organised forms of opposition, both local and national.

The adoption of the Freedom Charter as the ANC's primary political and economic programme represented two important developments: first, it codified the ANC's commitment to an accommodationist strategic approach to national liberation. Strategically prioritising a multi-class character to the struggle for national liberation (codifying what can only be called consensual politics), the Charter provided the logical foundation for a strategy of ideological and class accommodation. The ANC 'was able persuasively to stress common overarching interests, while blunting and even suppressing differences' (Marais, *Business Day*, 18 September 1991). The concept of the 'people' came to be seen primarily as constituent of all social classes divided along racial lines. National liberation was separated from social liberation. Racially defined national liberation assumed centre-stage and was to guide the ANC's approach henceforth.

Second, it represented a particular ideological 'party line'. Despite the legitimate claims (and the bent of the language in the Charter) by the ANC Alliance that they constituted a 'national movement', the Charter was the specific programmatic reflection of a political organisation seeking a prominent role in governing the country (that is, a party). The conscious fusion of this party programme with an all-inclusive national 'will' provided the ANC with the basis to claim a national mandate, not subject to the scrutiny and democratic processes associated with the principle of popular, mass-based party politics.

The demands of the Charter did offer an alternative to apartheid and provided an important rallying point for opposition to it. However, in its desire to gather all social forces into its fold, the Congress Alliance left much of the Charter open to widespread interpretation. So, for example, the clause demanding that the 'people shall share in the country's wealth' has been interpreted in a host of ways: the apartheid state, and subsequently much of the black working class and unemployed, have seen the clause as meaning the appropriation of large-scale private capital to a new majority-controlled state; some South African socialists have seen visions of worker-controlled 'people's' committees in alliance with a friendly state running the economy; many nationalists have foreseen a 'mixed economy' in which both the state and private capital share the driver's seat, redistributing resources to correct apartheid imbalances, and so on.

Similarly, the demand that 'the people shall govern' was open to ambiguous interpretation. For the ANC the word 'people' was understood to mean all those with an interest, whatever the motivations, in ending apartheid. In a 1956 article in the South African journal *Liberation*, Nelson Mandela confirmed such an understanding:

> The Charter does not contemplate [socialist] economic and political changes. Its declaration 'The People shall govern' visualises the transfer of power not to any single social class but to all the people of the country, be they workers, peasants, professionals, or petty bourgeoisie. (Pomeroy, 1986, p. 187)

This ambiguity in the Charter's clauses meant that the ANC Alliance could claim that their strategic approach was simultaneously a predominantly nationalist anti-apartheid umbrella for all social forces and a revolutionary struggle for radical socioeconomic transformation. The main problem was that the ANC's desired end, as expressed by Mandela, contained no requirement for the means needed to fulfil the second claim (that is, providing organisational and ideological content to the struggle of the only social force capable of forcing such radical change – the black working class).

It was the combination of a relatively unorganised, disparate and tired working class and the chosen strategies of the ANC that weakened any possible 'leading role' for the working class. The formation of the South African Congress of Trade Unions in 1955, and its subsequent membership in the Congress Alliance, was heralded by the Alliance as a practical expression of the commitment to working-class organisation and activity. However real this 'commitment' was, the reality of the formation of SACTU and the subsequent politics of its leadership was that of an adjunct trade union affiliate to the Congress Alliance – the trade union wing of a political 'party'.

The adoption of the Freedom Charter was not well received by the apartheid government. Seen as confirmation that the ANC (controlled by 'white communists') was bent on the 'violent overthrow' of the state, the Charter launched the apartheid machinery into a new round of activity. Utilising the Native Labour Act of 1953 the apartheid state began to arrest labour leaders and concerted attempts were made to limit the scope of activity of labour resistance. Pass laws were enforced with greater zeal and effectiveness and the white authorities vigorously pursued the ethnic fragmentation and control of the non-white population under the Group Areas Act (adopted in 1950). In its attack on the Congress Alliance the state arrested almost the entire leadership in 1956, charging them with treason for the attempted overthrow of the government. This set in motion the infamous Treason Trial in which over 100 leaders of the Congress Alliance – including all the leading figures in the ANC such as Nelson Mandela and Walter

Sisulu – were put on trial by the apartheid state. The trial dragged on until 1960, culminating in almost all of the senior leadership being found not guilty for lack of evidence.

Containing Mass Militancy

The apartheid onslaught was generally ignored by the international community. Multinational corporations were quite content to invest in the mining sector and the expanding industrial sector as long as the environment remained stable and profits kept rolling in. Major Western governments prioritised the apartheid state's strategic anti-communist appeal over any moral concern for apartheid policies (McKinley, 1986, pp. 9–10).

In response to both the apartheid state's offensive and local socioeconomic conditions there was a noticeable upsurge in oppositional activity. Boycotts, limited strike action, stay-aways, anti-pass actions, rural revolts and public demonstrations all took place during the late 1950s. Women once again played a major role in this activity as did the largely forgotten rural communities. What was noticeable was that much of this activity took place without a great deal of direction from the ANC. Local organisations, many affiliated or sympathetic to the Congress Alliance, showed immense resourcefulness and courage in the face of heavy-handed state repression. There were many factors that led to the lack of ANC involvement, among them the leadership's general absence as a result of the Treason Trial. But it was once again the ANC Alliance's strategic priorities – accommodating a wide range of ideological and class forces – that played a major role.

Underlying much of the ANC's approach was the decision to woo white liberal support for the anti-apartheid stance of the Alliance. As part of this accommodationist approach the ANC decided to support the (white) parliamentary opposition parties, the United Party and Labour Party, in the 1958 all-white elections. Fearing the alienating effects on white liberal and middle-class opinion, and seeking to preserve the unity of broad social forces within the Alliance, the ANC leadership continually sought to limit the scope of mass militancy. Going so far as to retreat from the demands contained in the Freedom Charter, and taking black mass support for granted, the ANC strategy helped create the conditions in which the designated masses were greatly weakened. Despite the ANC's efforts, the National Party won a majority in the elections, the white opposition was severely mauled and militant action by the black working class and other mass forces was dealt a body blow.

An example of this approach is the Alexandra bus boycott, Alexandra being one of the oldest and poorest black townships in Johannesburg. Although varying accounts of this boycott have been offered, what is not in dispute is the lack of ANC grassroots involvement and the controversial role it played in 'settling' the boycott by calling for a compromise with the state machinery.

None of these events deterred the ANC from its continued commitment to an all-inclusive national liberation, cast within a decidedly liberal democratic strategic framework. At the 1958 annual conference the ANC adopted a Constitution in which the 'Aims and Objects' of its struggle were:

> to unite the African people in a powerful and effective instrument to secure their own complete liberation from all forms of discrimination and national oppression; to promote and protect the interests of the African people in all matters ... to strive for the attainment of universal adult suffrage and the creation of a united and democratic S.A. on principles outlined in the freedom charter; and to support the cause of national liberation and right to independence of nations in Africa and the rest of the world. (ANC Constitution, 1958)

By the end of the 1950s, and despite numerous setbacks, the ANC had achieved success on numerous fronts: raising its liberation profile; forging a broad alliance of social forces to confront apartheid; and adopting a progressive document with degrees of radical potential. However, it had also helped create conditions in which the possibilities of transcending accommodationist politics were made extremely difficult. The militant struggles of the black working class and other sections of the oppressed majority did not have a chance against the ANC and the apartheid state, even if other more structural factors had played a role in their defeat.

The ANC, all denials to the contrary, was firmly planted in a strategy of seeking national liberation through social forces whose interests were diametrically opposed to anything other than limited political and economic reform. The mutations, rationalisations and consequences of this strategy form the essence of the ANC's externalised struggle, which was a great deal closer to being realised than anyone expected at the end of the 1950s.

2

National Liberation of a Special Type
(1960–75)

> Insofar as a victorious revolution will radically change the
> relation not only between the classes but also between the races
> ... thus far will the social revolution in South Africa also have
> a national character. The historic weapon of national liberation
> can be only the class struggle.
>
> Leon Trotsky[1]

In this chapter, the immediate events before the banning of the ANC
and SACP are central to an analysis of the reactive turn to armed
struggle. This turn was born of a historical failure to organise and
mobilise around the actual and potential militancy of the masses
and the adoption of a politics of despair, both of which marked a
strategic move away from the masses. The resultant externalisation situated the foundation of the liberation struggle, both in
content and context, outside the mass of the movement's own
constituency.

The adoption of the Communist Party-inspired two-stage
colonialism of a special type (CST) theory located the fight for South
Africa's national liberation squarely within traditional anti-colonial
struggles which effectively sidelined specific working-class struggle
and organisation. Armed struggle was now to be used as a new
pressure tactic for a larger accommodationist strategy that would
increasingly rely on international conditions and actors for its
sustenance, pointing the way to a consistent logic and practice of
an ANC-led struggle for national liberation.

Confirming the Strategic Dead-End

At the beginning of the 1960s the ANC once again found itself
lagging behind the militancy of the masses. Many people continued
to sustain substantial levels of resistance. For example, during
1959–60 women in Natal embarked on protests against a whole
range of apartheid-induced conditions, with state-run beer halls
(which threatened their home-brewing industry) as their main
target. Their anger spilled over into acts of violence (Fine and Davis,
1990, p. 217), which the ANC condemned while attempting to find

compromise solutions with the authorities. Similarly, in several rural areas (Zeerust, Sekhukhuneland and Pondoland) people battled against the apartheid machinery over issues ranging from cattle-culling to forced resettlement. While the ANC generally supported these struggles they did so from a distance. There was little ANC presence in the rural areas – which the organisation had generally ignored – and without any widespread support for rural struggles their revolts were much more easily crushed by the massive machinery of state repression.

The case of the Pondoland uprising is important for several reasons in that it revealed the militancy of the rural areas and people's willingness to resort to violence against the apartheid system; it clearly unmasked the ANC's lack of organisation in the rural areas (a weakness that was to remain with the ANC throughout); and it showed that unless and until there was a strategy that combined rural and urban, local and national struggles, the apartheid state would not face a crisis of survival.

Although the ANC called for a nationwide anti-pass campaign in 1959 this failed to materialise in any meaningful way, and in many areas the newly formed Pan Africanist Congress (PAC) took the lead. There have been conflicting accounts over whether the PAC usurped the ANC's existing anti-pass campaign, with ANC historians and sympathisers claiming that the PAC's call pre-empted what would have been a carefully planned and successful nationwide ANC campaign. While there is every reason to believe that the PAC's campaign relied on spontaneous action, the fact is that the ANC was once again seen to be lagging behind the mood of the people.

The PAC had only recently been formed by a number of ANC Youth League members who had resigned over what they saw as the undue influence of communists and non-blacks in the struggle for 'African' liberation. Borrowing from what they saw as the struggle for pan-Africanism, propagated by such African leaders as Kwame Nkrumah of Ghana, the PAC adopted the slogan 'Africa for the Africans' and argued for a more confrontational approach to the apartheid regime.

As its first attempt to contest the liberation landscape, the PAC, under its leader Robert Sobukwe, called for mass defiance against the pass laws on the day of the campaign's launch, 21 March 1960. Large crowds gathered at police stations in Evaton, Sharpeville (near Johannesburg) and Langa (near Cape Town) to protest. Police opened fire on the demonstrators at all three locations killing an estimated 100 people and injuring several hundred more. Sharpeville was the scene of the greatest slaughter.

The response of the black population was swift. Rioting broke out in many parts of the country, and demonstrations and marches took place in many of the larger urban areas. The ANC called for a day of mourning/stay-away on 28 March in response to this upsurge – a call that was met with widespread support. However, many workers and rural dwellers, independent of the ANC campaign, went further by embarking on mass strikes and indefinite stay-aways. The apartheid state's response to these actions included the imposition of a state of emergency, followed by mass arrests and the use of violence against resisters. It was only after much of this resistance had been effectively crushed by the state – lacking as it did any national coordination or direction – that the ANC stepped in and issued a call for a nationwide stay-away on 19 April to express its opposition to the apartheid state's actions.

This failed however, as the ANC's constituency was not prepared to embark on a spontaneous stay-away when it was still reeling from the wounds inflicted by the apartheid state's iron fist approach. In addition, the ANC had not provided strong leadership during the initial period after Sharpeville, and another stay-away call was not particularly helpful, nor was there any indication that it would have much effect on the decisions and activities of the state.

While it is true that many of the top cadres of the ANC were still involved in the Treason Trial, this could not excuse their lack of strategic direction and organisation. When the uprisings began, the ANC was incapable of leading and directing them. The organisation recoiled from the attendant militancy and its implications for the movement's chosen strategy – limited, non-violent and carefully planned acts of pressure which relied more on the favourable response of the perceived enemy than on the people the ANC purported to represent.

Sharpeville and its aftermath brought unprecedented turmoil to South Africa. The state had to contend with internal revolt, and was also faced for the first time with widespread international condemnation for its brutal measures. International investors and multinational corporations became jittery and temporarily withdrew substantial amounts of capital from the country. By one account, South Africa's foreign reserves were depleted by nearly 50 per cent (Milkman, 1982, p. 437). In spite of this the state – now under the leadership of Prime Minister Hendrik Verwoerd – chose the path of increased repression and consolidation by banning the ANC and PAC, declaring that South Africa would break from the Commonwealth and become a republic, and proceeding with its plan to entrench the apartheid system further.

The decision to take this path was understandable under the circumstances. Black opposition organisations were weak, international moral condemnation was just that, and international capital could be counted on to assist as soon as the internal situation was once again 'stable'. Indeed, the apartheid state was not disappointed on the last count. Revealing clearly the substance of their 'moral outrage', American corporations increased direct investments by US$23 million and American finance capital made loans of US$85 million to the government during the latter half of 1960 (Milkman, 1982, p. 437).

For its part, the ANC made one last attempt to try to persuade the government of the error of its ways. Convening an 'All in Africa Conference' for 25–26 March 1961, it demanded that the government convene a 'sovereign national convention' representative of all South Africans in order to 'work out solutions which would seek to preserve and safeguard the interests of all sections of the population' (Meli, 1988, p. 141). The conference demanded that this convention meet by 31 May 1961, failing which mass demonstrations would take place from 29 to 31 May to coincide with South Africa's declaration as a republic. The government did not respond.

As a result, and under the overall direction of Nelson Mandela, the protest went ahead as planned but was called off after the first day. Claiming that 'the strike was not the national success I had hoped for', Mandela curiously concluded by saying that 'this closes a chapter in our methods of political action' (Karis and Carter, 1973, p. 364). Exactly why Mandela made this statement is still subject to debate. He and other ANC leaders had simultaneously praised the protest as a success and denigrated it as an indication that such protest 'could no longer work'. It became obvious that a new tactical direction, no longer exclusively non-violent, was imminent.

Turning Away from a Mass Base

Shortly after the Republic Day failure an armed organisation, Umkhonto We Sizwe (better known as MK – 'Spear of the Nation'), was formed by individuals within the ANC. When the combination of events that preceded MK's formation is analysed it becomes clear what lay behind Mandela's statement and the subsequent turn to armed struggle:

1. Successful armed struggles had recently triumphed in Algeria and Cuba, and this proved a source of inspiration for many South Africans. The success of Fidel Castro and his small band of guerrillas along with the writings of Che Guevara greatly influenced ANC Alliance members. Guevara suggested that dedicated revolutionaries could create the conditions for overthrowing the state through armed struggle and this was very appealing in the circumstances in which the ANC found itself.
2. ANC leaders had been deeply affected by the armed rural uprising in Pondoland. Nelson Mandela, Walter Sisulu, Oliver

Tambo and Govan Mbeki were all from the region where the revolt took place, and had been distressed to see the inability of the ANC to respond effectively to the peasants' request for arms. This uprising, in combination with other violent acts, led many in the leadership to see a growing gap between their pacifism and what they saw as the readiness of the masses to resort to violence.

3. The ANC knew that the PAC and its armed wing, Poqo, as well as the newly formed National Committee of Liberation (made up of various radicals and Trotskyists), were gearing up for armed struggle. It therefore feared it would be outflanked.

4. At its December 1960 congress the reconstituted and (renamed) South African Communist Party (SACP) had resolved in favour of a campaign of economic sabotage to precede guerrilla warfare (Fine and Davis, 1990, p. 231). SACP members, all active in the Alliance, no doubt influenced ANC leaders, and the eventual decision to launch MK was taken by a group of individual leaders rather than the ANC organisationally.

5. The failure of years of non-violent accommodationism had given rise to what has come to be known as a 'politics of despair', the effect of which was to 'leave people behind without any continuity in struggle' (Hirson, 1992, personal interview). A switch to armed struggle seemed the only option left, something that has been confirmed by subsequent ANC historical explanation.[2]

6. Much of the ANC Alliance leadership perceived that South Africa was becoming isolated internationally and that this development had put the apartheid state in a severe economic and political crisis. They also saw 'imperialism' as being on the retreat elsewhere in Africa and thus decided to take advantage of such a 'ripening' situation (Slovo, 1976, p. 181).

The last point illustrates the short-sightedness of the movement's assessment of both imperialism and the role of international capital. Although there had been the withdrawal of some capital after Sharpeville, accompanied by the moral condemnation of apartheid, the main Western powers, in particular the US and UK, had simply been biding their time. Once it became clear that the apartheid state had effectively crushed the post-Sharpeville resistance and created, once again, a 'stable', investment-friendly environment, international support resumed with increased vigour. For example, US trade with South Africa (exports) rose by 33 per cent between 1963 and 1965 (McKinley, 1986, pp. 10–11).

MK was officially launched on 16 December 1961 and within months had carried out sabotage actions in three of South Africa's major cities – Johannesburg, Cape Town and Durban. Its inaugural manifesto declared that there

> comes a time in the life of any nation when there remain only two choices: submit or fight. That time has now come to South Africa. We shall not submit and we have no choice but to hit back by all means within our power in defence of our people, our future and our freedom. (ANC, 1991d, p. 5)

Although MK claimed to operate under the political guidance of the national liberation movement, it was in fact composed of leading ANC and SACP members who were acting in what they, as individuals, believed to be the best interests of the liberation struggle. In fact, it was not until the October 1962 Lobatse Conference, so-called for the small town in neighbouring Botswana in which it was held, that MK officially became recognised as the military wing of the ANC.

The initial sabotage campaign of MK was limited to strikes against 'things that represented the economy like pylons ... and things that represented oppression like pass offices' (ANC, 1991d, p. 10). However, the efforts of MK were severely curtailed by lack of resources and military know-how. Recounting these early days of sabotage, Ronnie Kasrils, one of the first MK recruits and later a leading MK commander, tells how MK units constructed homemade bombs using condoms and gelatin capsules as timing devices (Kasrils, 1993, pp. 39–40). The sabotage campaign had little effect militarily on the apartheid state and its machinery, although it did create sensational media headlines and raised the expectations of much of the black population.

During the months after its inception, the MK leadership (mostly senior ANC and SACP leaders) attempted to secure international support for the new armed struggle. It was in this regard that the SACP proved particularly important to the ANC. The SACP already had extensive contacts with the USSR and other friendly Soviet bloc countries which were the only potentially reliable sources of military hardware and financial support. MK leaders, including Nelson Mandela and Joe Slovo (a leading SACP member), went abroad to seek assistance, visiting East Germany, Algeria, Ghana, Tanzania and Zambia. Oliver Tambo, who had been sent outside the country soon after the ANC's banning to canvass support, succeeded in setting up an external headquarters/mission for the ANC in Dar es Salaam, Tanzania.[3]

This initial process of externalisation was beset by severe problems, both strategic and logistic. While the majority of the leadership remained under cover within South Africa, a few individuals were attempting to secure a launching pad for external guerrilla struggle far from the borders of South Africa. The only possible sites for such bases, as in the case of Tanzania, were not only far from South Africa but were also under severe constraints as newly independent nations in a Cold War world where political and economic pressure from Western powers sought to curtail any support for liberation movements. In such geopolitical conditions, when combined with the general administrative and strategic unpreparedness of the ANC and SACP to launch an armed struggle with domestic and international components, the chances of success were minimal.

Before MK was able to make any real progress in consolidating itself abroad, Nelson Mandela, who had secretly returned to South Africa after leaving the country in early 1962, was arrested in August 1962. It is a well-known fact that he was not to enjoy freedom for almost 28 years. This was a major blow to both MK, in which he played a leading role, and the ANC. In early 1963, almost the entire internal leadership of the ANC (also MK) was arrested at Rivonia by the South African police; subsequently most were sentenced to life imprisonment. The circumstances surrounding the Rivonia farmhouse arrests, where MK leaders were coming and going almost at will, where there were far too many people with knowledge of the location and key plans, and where strategic documents were left unsecured, were indicative of MK's lack of military professionalism and command and control structures – a situation of which the apartheid state's intelligence services took full advantage.

When the Rivonia farmhouse was raided numerous papers were found, including the 'Mayibuye Plan'. This document revealed that MK was planning a sustained guerrilla war financed and operating from outside the country. It was hoped that this would spark an internal uprising and crisis, which would lead to liberation. One of the methods contemplated was the use of planes to drop leaflets calling on the people to rise up in struggle. Cuba was cited as a model in this regard.

Although the Mayibuye Plan has subsequently been criticised as hopelessly adventurist and utopian, its basic outlines were to be followed once the ANC had set up in exile. Many ANC leaders and activists, including Slovo, later argued that the objective conditions present in 1962/63 were not properly appreciated; however, none has ever seemed to question the strategic correctness of the Plan.

Throughout this period the ANC's programme of mass struggle virtually ceased to exist inside the country. Although the Lobatse Conference reaffirmed the emphasis on mass action, most efforts were being directed towards the nascent armed struggle and international support. The Conference instructed the internal ANC, 'as a matter of urgency', to 'carry out the national programme of political education' and to implement 'the "M" Plan (the "Mandela Plan" of house-to-house, street-to-street cell organisation)' (Meli, 1988, p. 153). However, these never took root and the ANC leadership resorted to its old tactic of attempting to stimulate mass struggle by its own example. Unlike the 1950s, these examples now consisted of acts of sabotage instead of non-violent civil disobedience. The sabotage campaign by its very character relied on highly secretive organisation and minimal involvement of the oppressed sectors of the population. Where those sectors could have been involved (for example, within the organised labour movement) the ANC leadership's style of centralised direction of campaigns seriously impeded potential action. Confirmation of this approach came from the Lobatse Conference report on trade unions which, while appealing for more coordination between the South African Congress of Trade Unions (SACTU) and the ANC, stressed that SACTU should be regarded as a 'department of our movement rather than a separate movement' (Meli, 1988, p. 153).

The stated intention of the ANC and MK was to reinforce and spur mass struggle, but the way in which armed struggle was adopted, conducted and justified made this almost impossible. The decision taken to turn to armed struggle had been unilateral, justified by the lack of peaceful and/or legal means that supposedly made the old tactics no longer feasible.[4] Whether or not this was the case, the justification ignored the continued possibilities of 'legal and peaceful' struggle on the one hand, and mass struggle (which was not 'legal') on the other. By ruling out the possibilities and potentialities of long-term internal mass mobilisation and organisation, and opting for armed propaganda (which, under the objective conditions pertaining at the time, logically could only end up being externally based) to stimulate the same, the ANC and SACP situated the context and content of their struggle outside the masses. Ben Turok noted perceptively that:

> sabotage had the effect of isolating the organised movement from the mass who felt unable to join in this new phase or even to defend the actionists when they were seized ... The sabotage campaign failed on the main count – it did not raise the level of action of the masses themselves ... they were left on the threshold, frustrated bystanders of a battle being waged on their behalf ... (Turok, 1973, p. 360)

The Descent into an Exile Laager[5]

In 1959 the former CPSA had reconstituted itself as an independent part of the ANC Alliance, changing its name to the South African Communist Party. Along with this rebirth came the argument that its main role was to lead the working class in the attainment of the national democratic revolution. However, the strategic and theoretical implications of this were not clearly spelt out until 1962. In that year, at a secret location in Johannesburg, a handful of activists held a clandestine SACP 'national conference'. At the conference the SACP adopted a new programme, *The Road to South African Freedom*, which was to remain the SACP's central policy document until the late 1980s (SACP, 1981, pp. 284–320). The programme was to be of seminal importance.

The programme set out the theoretical and practical approach of the SACP towards apartheid, which it characterised as 'colonialism of a special type'. It argued that apartheid emanated from the era of monopoly capitalism and that South Africa reflected 'a combination of the worst features of imperialism and colonialism within a single national frontier' in which black South Africa was a colony of white South Africa. As the African population was seen as having 'no acute or antagonistic class divisions at present', it was only logical that the immediate task was to fight for the national liberation of the 'colonised'. This task would be carried out through a 'national democratic revolution' with the multi-class liberation movement as the main vehicle, but with the working class (the SACP being its vanguard) constituting the leading revolutionary force within it. Since not all classes had an objective interest in fundamental transformation of a post-apartheid South Africa, the working class's leading role would ensure that the struggle could be extended towards socialism. Thus the struggle had two stages: the first for a national democratic state, the second for socialism.

The argument by the SACP for a 'national democratic revolution' can be linked directly to the call by the Comintern (the international communist organisation headed by the USSR) in 1928 for an 'independent native republic'. The singularity of the SACP formulation was to place this within a specifically South African framework. And yet, the SACP had always followed the directives coming from Moscow (until the collapse of the USSR) – a tradition that proved both ideologically and organisationally debilitating.

Situating the strategic direction of the struggle within this kind of framework led to the perennial ascendancy of national struggle over that of class. What the SACP formulation meant was that the old 'people's front' strategy would be transplanted from a purely non-violent terrain to that of an internationalised guerrilla campaign. The struggles of the working class, directed as they were from an externally based guerrilla movement, would thus have to be aimed at servicing broad class coalitions in order to achieve the most immediate and important task of a 'national democratic revolution'. As part of this approach, armed struggle would thus act as a tactical pressure point (armed propaganda) for the larger macro-strategy of a negotiated liberation.

Most observers of ANC and SACP strategy locate the overt turn to a path of negotiation in late 1989 when the ANC issued its Constitutional Guidelines. While these Guidelines were certainly the first public confirmation of this stance, the logic of the entire strategic approach since 1961/63 had pointed in the direction of a negotiated outcome. This might not have been a conscious realisation among the leadership at the time, but it surely did not escape those who formulated the Guidelines as a strategic and tactical approach.

The separation of the struggle into that of class and racial liberation also ensured that the powerful class forces (domestic and international), whose self-interest would eventually lead them to seek a deracialised capitalism, would play a leading role in finding a solution – which certainly would not be the armed overthrow of the state. Though an armed seizure of power underlay the commitment and activities of the thousands who joined the external guerrilla forces, serious questions need to be raised about the intentions of leadership. Indeed, in an interview given in 1990 MK commander Ronnie Kasrils stated: 'There are revolutionary movements which, at their foundation, addressed the question of seizing state power. These immediately recognised and analysed the use of state power and the need to develop a force to seize state power. With us that was not the ethos' (Kasrils, 1990, p. 8).

Given such an approach, it was not surprising that the ANC and SACP leadership were convinced that their strategic choices would bring about national liberation whereby power would be transferred into the hands of the people. Writing in mid-1963 the SACP claimed:

> from the viewpoint of the historical process, the South African regime is steadily and swiftly being driven into a position of isolation, in which the armaments, capital and other forms of material and moral support which sustain it from abroad will one after another be cut short ... Even more important, inside South Africa itself – in spite of the massive-appearing and ever-growing state machine of domination and repression – the balance of forces is steadily changing in favour of the people and their liberation forces, and against the oppressing minority. (SACP, 1963, pp. 3–18)

And yet by the mid-1960s the conditions for the liberation struggle were anything but ripe. The apartheid state had succeeded virtually in wiping out the internal remnants of an organised ANC underground, as well as showing brutal efficiency in suppressing labour and local community struggles. The external liberation movement had yet to launch any kind of serious guerrilla activity and had slipped into a moribund state. MK recruits in training camps became disenchanted with the lack of military activity and generally poor conditions. Recruits certainly saw very little proactive contact with the internal situation. An ill-conceived attempt by MK leadership to infiltrate armed units into South Africa – the 'Wankie Campaign' (so-called after the Rhodesian 'Wankie' game reserve through which the units passed alongside Zimbabwe African People's Union guerrillas) – failed dismally. As one Wankie Campaign veteran put it: 'There was no longer any direction, there was general confusion and unwillingness to discuss the issues of revolution' (Lodge, 1983, p. 300).

Fitting onto the International Chessboard

The area where the exiled liberation movement did achieve some success was in gaining international support. On the one side of the Cold War coin the USSR, through the SACP, began to provide some material and military support. Even at this early stage the USSR was looking at the long-term benefits of having another national liberation struggle with which to play out its Cold War rivalry with the United States. Though there might have been a degree of 'socialist' and 'liberatory' camaraderie with the ANC and SACP (something that was felt closely by the South Africans), the record of the USSR's support for national liberation struggles around the world suggests that its main aim in supporting the South African movement was not concern with liberation, but rather with the addition of another ally. Examples would be the character of Soviet support in countries such as Mozambique, Somalia, Ethiopia and Vietnam. Many of the methods and policies of Soviet support revolved more around the military-industrial and domestic elite-power needs of the USSR than principled solidarity with oppressed peoples.

Given the parlous state of the ANC's organisational capabilities, guerrilla campaign and material well-being, it is not surprising that the ANC turned to foreign governments and international organisations for sustenance. Thus from a very early stage in its strategy of externalisation, the ANC (and to a lesser extent the SACP) devoted substantial time and effort to diplomacy.

The consequences of operating in this kind of environment were numerous. They included:

- the adoption of 'diplomatic habits' by the leadership (encouraged by friendly treatment from certain foreign governments). This had the potential to fuel 'escapist illusions' about the strength and importance of the movements that the

leadership represented, which in turn threatened to isolate the leadership socially from the rank and file;
- the search for support from foreign sources which could overshadow the existence of active membership within the country;
- the possibilities of focusing political energy around 'hairsplitting doctrinal disputes' and thus encouraging internal conflict centred around factionalism and personality (Lodge, 1983, pp. 295–6);
- the tendency towards a process of ideological osmosis, whereby reliance on international support could bring ideas and pressures that gradually undermine the initial principles of struggle;
- the potential for over-reliance on foreign support which could blind the movement to the differences between the principles of their struggle and the agenda of erstwhile supporters.

With the material and financial support provided by the USSR and its Eastern European allies, the ANC was able to establish a modest presence in Tanzania with the bulk of recruits situated in four camps around the country. The ANC was also beginning to have some success in attracting the support of the Scandinavian countries (particularly Sweden). In addition, most of the SACP leadership and structures were located in London at this time and the contacts with the British Communist Party and other organisations were to lead to the establishment of the British Anti-Apartheid Movement (AAM), which spawned a global network of similar anti-apartheid movements. On the African continent, the ANC relied on friendly but cash-strapped African governments (Tanzania and later Zambia and Angola) for bases. South Africa's 'other' liberation movement, the PAC, was not as well connected as the ANC, and throughout its exile was to experience severe financial problems owing to its over-reliance on pan-African support.

On the other side of the Cold War coin, the apartheid state in South Africa once again became an investment haven and a much needed ally of the West in the ongoing Cold War. It was rewarded accordingly. Between 1961 and 1965 corporate investment from the United States averaged over US$33 million per year, with much needed capital equipment channelled to the apartheid economy (Milkman, 1982, p. 437).

Despite the ANC's efforts to isolate the apartheid state internationally through the imposition of an arms embargo, its implementation was uneven and had little effect on South Africa's military capacity. Indeed, the extent of imperialism's realpolitik approach to the South African 'problem' was revealed in the proactive strategic support given to the apartheid state by the US:

political and trade relations expanded, and military hardware provided 'for defense against external threats' in exchange for strategic access in the form of satellite stations and use of port facilities (Danaher, 1985, p. 79). Apart from the efforts of the small progressive sections of their populations, both the US and Britain treated the ANC and SACP as revolutionary minnows, preferring for the time to leave the 'armed struggle' problem to their apartheid allies.

Nationalism Ascendant

On 25 April 1969 in Morogoro, Tanzania, the ANC held its Third Consultative Congress. The conference lasted seven days and most of the delegates were members of MK. Much of the conference debate centred on the need for organisational and leadership reforms and as a result the decision was made to establish an internal commission to hear grievances, as well as an oath and code of behaviour. It was decided further that MK and all military affairs would now come under the responsibility of a Revolutionary Council, subordinate only to the National Executive. On the policy front the conference took the decision after much debate to open ANC membership to all races. Although it was decided that these 'non-black' members could not belong to the National Executive, there was still strong opposition from several leading ANC members.

As a result of this decision, Joe Slovo, Yusuf Dadoo and Reg September (all SACP members and all non-black) were voted onto the new Revolutionary Council. The SACP had long pushed for a more cohesive relationship between the ANC and its allied organisations, and the membership decision, vigorously backed by SACP members and leaders at the conference, was a victory for the party. More importantly, though, was the adoption by the conference of a new 'Revolutionary Programme', commonly known as the 'Strategy and Tactics' document.

Since the publication of the 1955 Freedom Charter the ANC had not produced a written policy and strategy document that took into account the completely new situation of being an exiled liberation movement. The 'Strategy and Tactics' document – sounding very much like the work of the SACP – began by stating that the South African liberation struggle was taking place 'within an international context of the transition to the Socialist system ... we in South Africa are part of the zone in which national liberation is the chief content of the struggle.' In placing the question of the seizure of power firmly at the strategic centre, it argued that 'it is surely a question of whether, in the given concrete situation, the course or policy advocated will aid or impede the prospects of the conquest of power'.

'Strategy and Tactics' went into some detail about the history of the armed struggle and the 'special' circumstances of South Africa which made guerrilla warfare both appropriate and necessary – both in the rural and urban areas. In a related document, 'Development of the South African Revolution', also produced at the conference, the primacy of armed struggle was linked to the rejection of reforms. This document stated that,

> there is not one single factor to justify any expectation that reform could even lead to any amelioration of our conditions. The only correct path for the oppressed national groups and their democratic supporters ... is armed revolutionary struggle. This is not altered by the problems and difficulties that confront us in developing the revolution. (de Braganca and Wallerstein, 1982, p. 73)

Assessing the 'strength and weakness' of the enemy, the 'Strategy and Tactics' document followed the classic guerrilla warfare scenario of weaker forces conducting a war of attrition against superior enemy forces, reminiscent of a Cuban-style struggle. Although it argued that the working class constitutes a 'distinct and reinforcing layer of our liberation and Socialism' (the only place in the document where the word 'socialism' is identified as a goal of struggle), the document made it clear that the thrust of the struggle should have a national focus. If there was any doubt of the strategic aims of the ANC it was answered in no uncertain terms:

> it is only the success of the national democratic revolution which – by destroying the existing social and economic relationships – will bring with it a correction of the historical injustices perpetrated against the indigenous majority and thus lay the basis for a new – and deeper internationalist – approach. Until then, the national sense of grievance is the most potent revolutionary force which must be harnessed. (Turok, 1980, pp. 145–57)

What the 'Strategy and Tactics' document represented, above all, was the ascendancy of the SACP's theoretical and practical vision of struggle within the ANC. Some seasoned observers such as Tom Lodge have disputed this, pointing to the 'welfare state capitalism' approach of the document and the 'conservative (and realistic) ideological' position of the ANC before and after Morogoro (1983, p. 301). The assumption that underlies Lodge's position is that the SACP represented a competing radical and revolutionary socialist ideology and that there were few, if any, important effects on the SACP and ANC stemming from the USSR's patronage. In fact, the entire theoretical framework for the SACP's strategic vision, codified at Morogoro, derived sustenance from Comintern formulations on the national liberation question.

While arguments such as Lodge's are most often made against those who charge that the ANC was subordinated to the control of the SACP (the 'conspiracy' theory), the reality is that the nationalist and welfare state capitalist outlook of the 'Strategy and Tactics' document was the logical manifestation of the SACP's own formulations. The disassociation of moderate nationalist and welfare capitalist strategies from the SACP itself ignores the fact that the SACP's strategic vision of a struggle for a 'national democratic revolution' as the first stage in the ultimate struggle for socialism embodied these very characteristics. Long-time ANC critic Neville Alexander makes the controversial argument that the SACP served only to 'strengthen the petit-bourgeois direction and character of the ANC', because of its analytical and organisational skills. In his words, the SACP gave the ANC a 'revolutionary image and legitimacy' (personal interview, June 1992).

After Morogoro, the ANC's top bodies took on a distinctly two-tiered appearance and approach to functions. The leadership of the new ANC National Executive Committee (NEC) resembled a who's who of early Youth Leaguers. Oliver Tambo was formally elected as President-General, Alfred Nzo as Secretary-General and Thomas Nkobi as Treasurer-General. Although the NEC was the highest decision-making body in the ANC, its main day-to-day tasks remained organisational and diplomatic. The new 'Revolutionary Council', with a majority SACP membership, took control of what had been identified as the ANC's main task: prosecuting the armed guerrilla struggle. Mention should also be made of the imprisoned leadership on Robben Island. Even though Mandela, Sisulu and others were separated from the daily running of the ANC and MK, they were to wield influence through the many jailed activists who went in and out of Robben Island, and when possible through written contact with the external leadership.[6]

Despite the organisational changes and 'new' strategic direction, the ANC's internal problems did not end. Internal bickering over the inclusion of non-Africans and the influence of the SACP within the ANC continued. This eventually resulted in a public feud and the expulsion of eight prominent ANC members for 'destabilising activities'. Although many of the criticisms had the air of personal grievance, the accusations of undemocratic decision-making and a general Stalinist atmosphere were more serious. That they were mostly dismissed with contempt was unfortunate, for the same accusations were to surface later with more serious consequences.

On the armed struggle front things were not much better. There were several partially successful attempts to infiltrate MK cadres across the Botswana border, the explosion of leaflet bombs in some major South African cities and at least one ill-fated plan to land guerrillas on the South African coast. Former MK commander Ronnie Kasrils subsequently told the story of how the movement bought an old boat to transport the party of guerrillas, but the plan was abandoned when the boat's engines failed off the Kenyan coast. The message to the internal contact was: 'Regret to inform you mother has died' (Kasrils, 1993, pp. 112–13). It was a far cry from the revolutionary guerrilla onslaught called for at Morogoro.

On the positive side the ANC could point to at least two successes: it had managed to hold itself together, which was, under the prevailing circumstances, no small achievement; and it was gradually succeeding in winning increased international support for itself and a growing anti-apartheid campaign. However, by the mid-1970s the ANC was reaping the bitter consequences of its chosen strategy and tactics: the externally based guerrilla war was yet to get off the ground; relationships between the leadership and rank and file were under strain; there was a near-complete lack of internal structures; and the apartheid state was not threatened, while domestic and international capital were enjoying the benefits of a relatively stable apartheid South Africa.

Nearly 15 years after its strategic decision to locate the centre of its liberation struggle within an externalised guerrilla campaign, the ANC was no closer to seizing power than it had been in the late 1950s. It was not without a degree of irony that the impetus for changing this situation was to come, not from the external ANC, but from renewed internal struggle.

3

From Soweto to Kabwe (1976–84)

> Masses do not of their own accord generate an ideology which
> provides true guidelines on the main direction of the struggle,
> or which makes them conscious of the necessity to create non-
> exploitative relations of production.
>
> Joe Slovo[1]

It is within the context of apartheid capitalism's emergent economic
crisis, beginning in the early 1970s, that the logic of ANC liberation
strategy becomes much clearer. The crisis of over-accumulation
and production, stemming from the combined limitations of
apartheid social engineering and capitalist relations of production,
produced both the objective and subjective conditions that presented
the ANC with the clear strategic challenge of giving its anti-
apartheid struggle a specifically anti-capitalist content. It was such
a strategy that could harness both the revolutionary power of the
working class and the broader struggle for national liberation. And
yet the ANC's strategic response served only to strengthen the
previously chosen path of an accommodationist, externalised
struggle, for, while widening the potential faultlines of apartheid
capitalism, it led to a consolidation of the ANC's 'united front'
(broadest coalition of forces) tactics, both internally and internationally. Ultimately, the way in which the ANC incorporated the
strategic challenges thrown up by the crisis of apartheid capitalism
substantively undermined the potential for mass struggle.

Gathering Crises

Slovo's statement at the head of this chapter encapsulates the
dynamic of the ANC's and SACP's approach to struggle during
the 1970s and early 1980s. Throughout this period, and in the midst
of the labour, student and community (for example, youth, women's
and civic associations) struggles inside South Africa, the ANC
continued to direct the liberation struggle from its external base.

By the early 1970s South Africa was beginning to experience the
problematic effects of apartheid capitalism. The historic division
of labour between well-paid, skilled white workers and low-wage
unskilled black workers had gradually been undermined by the

demands of expanding South African capitalism. Black workers were no longer confined to predominantly migrant unskilled labour, not because of any change of heart by white capital, but because of the new demands of the system. There had been tremendous growth of the black working class: between 1951 and 1980 the number of Africans employed in manufacturing rose from 360,000 to 1,103,000, and in mining from 449,000 to 768,000. Growth, particularly in the manufacturing sector, had been greatest in the mid- to late 1960s (Callinicos, 1986, p. 28).

Large-scale foreign investment during the 1960s, the subsequent take-off in the manufacturing sector and the need of the apartheid state to create ever-expanding economic opportunities for its white supporters all contributed to a growing internal crisis by placing contradictory political and socioeconomic demands on a state that was unwilling and unable to adapt. This was not just a political crisis engendered by apartheid, but a structural economic crisis of over-accumulation and production. Such a crisis could not be solved by short-term political and/or economic reform; revolutionary change was needed.

In short, the South African economy had reached a point where the (recently dominant) manufacturing sector was producing far too many luxury consumer goods for the limited South African market (limited further by the artificial apartheid barriers to consumption such as low wages for the majority). The resultant growth of financial capital was not channelled into production but rather turned to new, previously unprecedented areas of speculation in its characteristic search for maximisation of profits (for example, by playing the stockmarket). Simultaneously, in their attempt to overcome this crisis, the apartheid state and domestic capital tried to corporatise labour, develop a black petit-bourgeois consumption class, streamline production (which led to mass unemployment) and find external avenues through which to channel their over-accumulated capital.

These attempts to mediate the crises were hampered not only by the active resistance of the oppressed sectors, who bore the brunt of such efforts, but also by the structural contradictions inherent in the process of capitalist production and accumulation. The confluence of these 'resistances' highlighted the need for a specifically anti-capitalist struggle directed at both the root causes and the symptoms of apartheid capitalism's exploitation. In other words, by itself the 'national' component of the liberation struggle could not (and cannot) fully address the class oppression suffered by the majority of South Africans.

Had the ANC attempted to translate the critiques of capitalism present in its own documents and (written) in the history of the South African struggle into practical strategies, they would have been better able to grasp the possibilities of mass grassroots struggle. Indeed, the bases of the struggles during the 1970s and 1980s, dominated as they were by the workers and the unemployed, were explicit responses not only to the ravages of apartheid, but to the crises engendered by the process of capitalist accumulation. Practical strategies that were confined to seeking the shortest possible route to national liberation (as the negotiations of that period were later referred to by ANC leaders) under the objective conditions that pertained could only see mass struggle as a tactical weapon; they could not provide a solid foundation for creating the possibilities for a 'full transfer of power to the people'. Such an assessment of the dialectic between struggle and structure (despite rhetoric to the contrary) led the ANC to approach the internal struggles of the 1970s and 1980s, not on the terms of those struggles, but rather on the terms of the ANC's narrow view of national liberation.

The rationale for the ANC approach included a verbal (intellectual) recognition of the capitalist basis of apartheid. No one was more lucid in explaining this than leading ANC and SACP member Joe Slovo. In order to do so, he gave intellectual and strategic primacy to the argument that the liberation struggle could only realistically concentrate its energies on an anti-apartheid terrain, thus, artificially (even if unwillingly) separating the struggle into its racial and class components. This approach was in the best tradition of the SACP's two-stage theory of revolution, and its logical consequence was to ignore the strategic need to develop a specifically anti-capitalist struggle.

Although the architects of apartheid capitalism and the externalised ANC wavered in their response to the gathering crisis, workers once again showed the way. In early 1973 tens of thousands of workers in the coastal city of Durban went on a spontaneous strike. Refusing to elect a leadership, enter into negotiations with their employers or affiliate themselves with any specific political or union organisation, the workers succeeded in gaining most of their wage demands (Lodge, 1983, pp. 327–8). Their example set off other nationwide struggles, though these met with a mixed response of repression and attempts at cooption. More importantly, the workers infused a new sense of struggle in the black population and a small but influential sector of whites, which was to lead to the formation of a new trade unionism outside the Alliance's political umbrella (Hemson, 1978).

Some of the more radical whites joined with workers to form new worker advisory organisations. It was through such organisations that a new type of independent 'workerist' union, concentrating on industrial unionism and shop-floor organisation, emerged. These unions (for example, the Metal and Allied Workers Union) eventually gathered together as the Federation of South African

Trade Unions (FOSATU) and were to go a long way in contesting the hegemony of 'political' unions like SACTU as being representative of South African workers. It was this 'workerist' direction that was to come into direct conflict with the ANC and SACP vision of worker organisations as subservient to the primacy of the political demands of the 'national democratic' struggle.

On another internal front there had been growing unrest amongst black students in the early 1970s over the poor quality of educational infrastructure, lack of opportunities for further education and the general abscence and the general lack of any coherent internal struggle. In the absence of any organised liberation movement structures, the students had formed their own representative bodies in the form of the South African Students Organisation (SASO), expanded later in 1972 into the Black People's Convention (BPC), and the Black Community Programmes (BCP). These new organisations were strongly influenced by a rejuvenated intellectual version of the Africanist tradition. Aptly named 'black consciousness', this new approach posited that the struggle against apartheid was primarily a battle of values and identity. SASO's manifesto declared that it worked for

> the liberation of the Black man first from psychological oppression by themselves through induced inferiority complex and secondly from physical oppression accruing out of living in white racist society ... (A. Marx, 1992, p. 52)

Concentrating their efforts on self-empowerment and upliftment, Black Consciousness Movement (BCM) bodies did not fundamentally threaten the immediate interests of the apartheid state. The emphasis of practical BCM politics was to focus on individual and collective expression of black pride, which could be realised through various social and community projects. While this approach had a longer-term potential to create and/or strengthen national struggles for political and economic liberation, there was little organisational cohesion or a coherent political strategy which would have assisted in the consolidation of (possible) psychological liberation by contesting the more immediate physical manifestations (i.e. institutions) of apartheid rule.

Even with its strategic limitations and lack of a mass base the BCM influenced an entire generation, particularly young black intellectuals and students from urban areas. It was this group which was to provide the externalised ANC with the means to resurrect the armed struggle and give a much needed injection of youthful militancy to the liberation struggle. The BCM structures, along with new labour formations, came to represent the main focus of internal struggle during the early to mid-1970s. For its part, the ANC literally stood on the sidelines, preoccupied with its own external problems and plans. However, there was some activity by those ANC members who were fresh from Robben Island (for example, Joe Gqabi), and the possibility of building underground structures by an MK detachment based in Lesotho led by Chris Hani was mooted (Ellis and Sechaba, 1992, pp. 72–3).

Meanwhile, throughout the 1970s the apartheid state continued to expand its apartheid programme by forcibly removing millions from the burgeoning urban black population to the bantustan wastelands (for example, Transkei and Venda), and arresting an equal number who showed dissent. Alongside this repression attempts were made at a more reformist approach. Grasping the need to deepen social, material and racial divisions among the non-white population in order to consolidate apartheid, the state began to provide limited political and economic opportunities to the small black middle class as well as the Coloured and Indian 'national groups'. This most often took the form of government subsidies to small and medium-sized business, increased access to credit facilities and the creation of local political and administrative bureaucracies ('self-run' community/township councils).

Such state-sponsored reform marked the beginning of a much more important process which was to characterise the contradictory agendas of South Africa's ruling class. By the mid-1970s some sectors of the ruling class had come to realise that in order to save capitalism the fundamentals of apartheid would have to be jettisoned. While the state was engaged in developing further its grand apartheid development plan, representatives of South African capital were stressing the need to promote class formation as fundamental to the very survival of capitalism itself. In 1976 Anton Rupert, chairman of the mega-conglomerate Anglo American, declared that 'we [capitalists] cannot survive unless we have a free market economy [and] a stable black middle class' (Pomeroy, 1986, p. 123). Although this realisation did not involve talks or negotiations with the ANC at the time, the externalised liberation movement was eventually to become central to this reform process. In the meantime domestic business responded to the crisis in apartheid capitalism by embarking on a programme of devaluing capital. This resulted in higher inflation rates, employee retrenchment, or redundancies (increasing the suffering of the already burdened majority) and increased monopolisation.

Such moves led to the creation of a social tinderbox. A spark was all that was needed to set it off.

Answered Prayers and Lost Opportunities

Besides the internal developments leading up to the events of 1976 there had been much activity on the international front which affected both the oppressed and oppressor in South Africa. For decades the apartheid state had enjoyed the security given by friendly colonial and racist white neighbours. So, the events of 1974–75 came as a body blow. After the fall of the fascist regime in Portugal in 1974, the new government rapidly set about granting independence to its colonies of Angola and Mozambique. In Mozambique the only serious liberation movement, Frelimo, formed the new government, while in Angola three competing movements, MPLA, FNLA, UNITA, jockeyed for power. Since both Frelimo and the MPLA (who were on the verge of taking power in Angola) were supported by the USSR, the apartheid state 'saw red'. In collusion with the United States it proceeded to back the 'pro-Western' FNLA and UNITA in Angola in a desperate attempt to prevent the MPLA from consolidating its imminent victory (Stockwell, 1978). The subsequent South African military incursion into Angola ended in a hasty retreat in the face of a combined MPLA/Cuban counter-offensive. This was both a severe setback to apartheid confidence and a great inspiration for black South Africans.

Despite these regional developments the apartheid authorities felt confident enough to expand their efforts at control at home. When the state decreed that Afrikaans was to be the medium of instruction (initially for mathematics and social studies) in black high schools, a small group of BCM-affiliated students in Soweto, organised under the banner of the South African Student Movement (SASM), responded with active resistance and small demonstrations. The national leadership of the BCM structures had little to do with these early demonstrations in early 1976, but after the state responded with violence, it took up the call for further action (A. Marx, 1992, pp. 66–7).

The vast majority of students involved in these activities had little or no connection with the externally-based national liberation movements. One of the 1976 activists, Murphy Morobe (later to become a major figure in the Alliance-aligned United Democratic Front, UDF), put it this way: 'we thought we were the first people to fight the government. We did not know about the Defiance campaign and the school boycotts in the 1950s' (Ellis and Sechaba, 1992, p. 83). The events that followed on 16 June took almost all the major organisations and the apartheid state by surprise. Emboldened by the radical rhetoric of black consciousness and the general climate of resistance that had developed since the 1973 strikes, and spurred on by the deteriorating socioeconomic situation, large numbers of students and urban dwellers went on the offensive. Six days after the first student demonstration a total of 136 people were officially listed as having been killed (A. Marx, 1992, p. 68).

Nevertheless, the apartheid state quickly doused the insurrectionary flames. It was aided by the lack of well-organised grassroots
structures to direct the anger and action. The uprising had thus
clearly revealed both the potential power and the severe limitations
of black consciousness 'ideology': at one level it had succeeded in
mitigating the subservient attitude it was so concerned to combat;
but on the other, it had no theoretical or strategic base from which
to organise and direct the resistance that followed. While the
externalised ANC possessed such a base, it had little internal
organisational presence. Although there were the beginnings of an
independent working-class movement that might fill this role, it
was still too weak and split by division over the 'national democratic'
question and the relationship to the externalised liberation
movement to take up the challenge.

An example of this division was revealed in the late 1970s infights
that erupted within SACTU (not unlike the wrangles that raged
in the 1930s and 1940s between Trotskyites and members of the
then CPSA over the direction and organisation of working-class
struggle). In the case of SACTU the principal battle-line was
drawn between two opposing perspectives. On the one side, there
were those directly allied to the ANC and SACP, who argued that
the 'national liberation' programme demanded that working-class
organisations should concentrate their energies on securing cadres
for the externalised movement and support the programme of
multi-class politics (SACTU, 1978). On the other, were those
who argued that an (overt) alliance with the ANC and SACP
would lead to the subservience of an independent working-class
politics to the broad multi-class demands of the ANC's national
liberation strategies, and its emphasis on guerrilla-induced
mobilisation ('The Workers' Movement and SACTU', undated).
It was to the ANC and SACP's discredit that they limited debate
and continued to be wholly convinced that independent worker
struggles should be left to their stagist post-'national democratic
revolution' phase of liberation. By doing so, the externalised
liberation movement helped (even if unwittingly) to create the
conditions for a truncated liberation.

What the 1976 uprising showed, once again, was the lack of
effective internal (underground) revolutionary organisation to
absorb and subsequently carry forward the militant struggle of the
masses. The leadership of the ANC continued to practise an
externalised strategic approach that was informed by a particularly
narrow interpretation of the possibilities under the prevailing
objective conditions; in effect, they did not trust the capabilities
and potential of grassroots struggle. Such an approach was not
conducive to sustainable internal organisation. Instead, the ANC
was waiting in the wings with its guerrillarist 'national democratic

revolution' vision. One estimate of the ANC/SACP presence inside South Africa at the time states that there were at most 50 formal units (presumably made up mostly of MK cadres and recruits) totalling 200 people (Barrell, 1990, p. 32).

However, encouraged by the internal upsurge in mass struggle and belatedly cognisant of the organisational gap that existed, the ANC began to recruit actively and to circulate propaganda. ANC literature, which had not been seen inside South Africa for a long time, was widely distributed, accompanied by the organisation's symbols (for example, logos). At the same time, the ANC began to encourage students and other activists to leave the country and join its armed MK wing – an exercise made easier by the large numbers who were already trying to escape detention. Indeed, many of the 1976 generation were to turn to the externalised ANC, not out of ideological or organisational affinity but from desperate necessity. Another source of ANC support was to come from the substantial numbers of BCM leaders and activists imprisoned on Robben Island which became known as the 'University', where activists 'graduated' under the tutelage of Nelson Mandela, Walter Sisulu and Govan Mbeki. It was these graduates who were to play leading roles in the UDF in the 1980s.

As people poured across South Africa's borders, it was the ANC that provided the only organisation capable of absorbing such an outflow. Its main external rival, the PAC, was hopelessly underfunded and disorganised and therefore unable to offer similar hospitality, although many of the BCM-influenced students were prime recruits for the PAC's Africanist image.

The ANC had a distinct advantage thanks to its access to substantial material and military support from the USSR, something the PAC never managed with its patron, China. Such support has often been assessed in a one-dimensional way by South African struggle historians and analysts, where the focus remains on its practical importance and advantages (for example, Lodge, 1983). What is not mentioned though, is the 'baggage' that can come with such support – methods of organisation and control. In the case of the ANC and SACP the influence of Stalinist methods and theory was to prove increasingly debilitating despite the benefits of access to substantial material resources. The USSR's influence was also shown in the propaganda of the externalised liberation movement which, on the international level, continued to mimic Soviet Cold War rhetoric. In a speech to the UN General Assembly soon after the 1976 uprising, ANC President-General Oliver Tambo reflected such influence thus:

> While imperialism ... predicates its own survival on the survival of the white minority regime ... the confrontation between the

liberation movement as a whole, on the one hand, and the forces of imperialism, on the other, cannot but grow sharper, for a strategy for the strengthening of the criminal apartheid regime is simultaneously a strategy for the destruction of the forces within South Africa that seek to bring about a genuinely popular change ... The same idea [of a non-radical solution] is conveyed in statements by representatives of the United States government. We take this to be a very categorical and clear statement by the world's leading imperialist power ... that it is prepared to accept only such a solution as would leave its interest in South Africa intact. Neither the African National Congress nor our people as a whole can ever accept such a solution.[2]

What Tambo did not appear to grasp, despite the obvious sincerity of his opposition to the recent role of the United States, was that his own organisation's strategy, heavily influenced as it was by Stalinism, threatened to move in the very direction stated as unacceptable – that is, a non-radical solution.

With new blood in its ranks alongside the high expectations of MK's increased guerrilla activities inside the country the ANC's main strategic focus, that of armed struggle, was faced with a major test. In its efforts to meet this the organisation formed the Operations Unit (OU), whose task it was to rejuvenate the movement's armed struggle as quickly as possible. This hastily convened unit was, however, to create major communication, coordination and strategic problems for MK. The Revolutionary Council (RC – responsible for the overall prosecution of armed struggle), the Politico-Military Strategy Commission (PMSC – responsible for reviewing ANC strategy and tactics) and another sub-body, the Internal Reconstruction and Development Unit (IRD – responsible for political work) were already in operation. With the formation of the OU it appeared that one hand did not necessarily know what the other was doing, and serious problems arose when carrying out joint military and political work, as called for in the ANC's strategic guidelines (Barrell, 1990, p. 32). Indeed, a meeting of the RC and the ANC NEC in 1978 emphasised the need to combine armed activity with legal and semi-legal internal activity in order to spur 'general mass uprisings' (Barrell, 1990, pp. 37–40). However, it took the ANC four years before its armed struggle registered substantially increased activity. During 1977–80 the guerrilla activities inside the country totalled 82 incidents, and in 1981–84 there was a total of 194 incidents (Lodge, 1988, p. 230). Much of the armed activity mirrored the sabotage campaign of the early 1960s, with small units attacking military and administrative targets.

The resurgence of armed activity had three main goals: first, to catalyse internal mass mobilisation and political activity centred on the ANC; second, to show that the ANC was the only serious liberation movement willing to engage the enemy and defend the people by force of arms; and third, to ensure the armed seizure of power. The degree to which the last goal was realistic or credible to the leadership is open to debate. Whatever the case, what is clear is that the majority of MK cadres and the broad mass inside South Africa took armed seizure of power seriously. As far as the other two (more practicable?) goals were concerned, by 1978 there had been some success with the second (aided by the absence of any competition), but the goal of spurring mass political struggle had proved elusive.

The ANC once again was a victim of its own misdirected strategies. Still clinging to the centrality of a guerrilla strategy designed to incite mass resistance and seize power, the organisation was blinded to the realities of its failure. The international and internal changes that the ANC saw as strengthening their strategy were, if anything, confirmation that an externalised guerrilla strategy could be little more than what it had become – armed propaganda.

The apartheid state was nowhere near being threatened militarily, the geopolitical obstacles were formidable and the internal conditions necessary for successful guerrilla-type operations were tenuous at best. The only change that seemed to be working in favour of the ANC was the growing anti-apartheid sentiment abroad. And yet, this success had little to do with the strategic success of a guerrilla insurgency supposedly aimed at overthrowing the enemy by force and ushering in a transformative national democratic revolution. For all the clearly stated proclamations of the inevitable correctness of its strategic formulations, the ANC's practice had not borne this out. The main problem was actually quite simple; the ANC leadership was not being honest – either to itself or to those it was leading.

Competing for Hearts and Minds

The voice of the mass democratic movement, headed by the ANC and its allies is winning the hearts and minds of growing numbers from amongst all the oppressed

ANC NEC statement (8 January 1982)[3]

By the early 1980s the ANC was confident that it had finally achieved the status it had always claimed – that of 'sole legitimate representative' of the South African oppressed. Although this claim was somewhat arrogant as well as dismissive of the complexities of the South African liberation struggle, the ANC certainly was holding centre-stage. Increased sabotage action, now conceptualised by the leadership as 'armed propaganda' and backed by dissemination of ANC iconography, plus the organisation's ample international support, had given the ANC a high profile.

The ANC's external presence had, by the early 1980s, become a giant exercise. Apart from the thousands of MK cadres in camps around the region, the organisation had a large educational complex in Tanzania (the Solomon Mahlungu Freedom College), administrative headquarters in Lusaka, several hundred ANC members studying at foreign universities and a diplomatic presence in over 30 countries, of which London was the most important.

On the strategic front, the chosen 'new' direction – mooted in 1978 – of merging armed and mass internal struggle, went public in 1982. A series of debates was published in the SACP's official journal *The African Communist*, which centred on the merits of 'arming the masses' and a 'people's war'. Such 'new' thinking no doubt played a role in the ANC's propaganda efforts, but as in the past practice belied theory: the hard reality was that the ANC was nowhere near building the kind of internal structures that could generate 'mass uprisings' and which might lead to an insurrectionary seizure of power. Instead, the ANC's campaign to win the 'hearts and minds' took on such an all-inclusive character and cast its net so widely as to make revolutionaries of anyone remotely cognisant of the inevitable downfall of apartheid, with the exception of the 'colonial settler regime'.

While the term 'colonial settler regime' is most often associated with the PAC, it is used here as indication of the interconnection between the ANC's practical politics and the PAC's philosophical allegiance to racial exclusivism. Although the ANC and its allies had a multiracial composition, the way in which the organisation pursued its goal of 'national democratic revolution' was infused with a predominantly racial logic. Since the ANC wanted to win the hearts and minds of anyone opposed to the apartheid system, the only serious enemy target had to be the white racists in power and those that actively supported them. By setting up the main fight as one between this racial enemy and its own agenda for national liberation (which other progressive forces could join), the ANC was, at the very least, unconsciously capitulating to a narrow, racially defined logic of liberation.

Meanwhile, within the previously predictable politics of the apartheid state some major shifts began to take place in the late 1970s. Spurred on by an increasingly jittery domestic capital, apartheid authorities sought ways to reform the system without any subsequent loss of political or social control. The new cabinet of P.W. Botha (National Party leader elected to the premiership in the 1978 elections) set out to do just that. Botha had come to power on the back of the security establishment which wanted to implement a 'total strategy' plan as a means of combating both 'revolutionary' resistance and winning the hearts and minds of non-whites through economic and political cooption.

The first shot in this strategic war was the formation of the Wiehahn Commission in 1979 to investigate labour relations and conditions. This was subsequently followed by recommendations for reform in trade union legislation, education and so-called influx control of the black urban population. The implementation of such reforms presented the apartheid state with myriad problems. The legalisation of trade union activity, increased access to skills enhancement and relaxation of controls over the movement and employment of the urban population provided the space for renewed resistance by both the black and white working class.

For the black working class the reforms allowed for a phenomenal growth of militant independent trade unionism, with the numbers of registered union members increasing from 220,000 in 1980 to 670,000 in 1983. These independent trade unions were, for the most part, separate from the Alliance-aligned SACTU, which consisted of unions such as the South African Allied Workers Union (SAAWU) and the General and Allied Workers Union (GAWU). By 1984 the independent unions included: the Federation of South African Trade Unions (FOSATU), a non-racial federation with nine affiliated unions comprising 106,000 members, and the Council of Unions of South Africa (CUSA), heavily influenced by black consciousness and with ten affiliated unions comprising 148,000 members and dominated by the National Union of Mineworkers (Callinicos, 1986, p. 29). For the white working class the reforms represented a direct threat to established privileges and gave them reason to question their traditional support for the National Party; they increasingly turned to more far-right options such as the newly formed breakaway from the National Party, the Herstigte Nasionale Party.

The main thrust of the Botha reform measures was designed to ease the pressure points within the apartheid capitalist system while still guaranteeing the essential features of white domination. In this, Botha and his securocrats[4] had received substantial support from international capital. Despite the international furore that followed the Soweto revolt, the apartheid state secured access to large amounts of capital, mainly through the International Monetary Fund (IMF). Between 1976 and 1982 the IMF 'loaned' almost 1.5 billion dollars to the apartheid state (Padayachee, 1987, p. 39).

None the less the apartheid state desperately needed to find internal allies and further attempts were made at cooption: thus, the Indian and Coloured communities were invited to join the Tricameral Parliament system in 1984; increased economic opportunities were extended to the small black middle class; and the recently created 'independent states' (Ciskei, Transkei, Venda, Bophutatswana), 'self-governing' homelands (Kwa-Zulu, KaNgwane, KwaNdebele, Lebowa, Gazankulu, Qwaqwa), and local municipal authorities were offered as the locus for petit-bourgeois, ethnically driven capital accumulation and limited political power.

Although these reforms catalysed resistance to the apartheid state, they also introduced powerful forces of cooption and encouraged division. The 'independent' and 'self-governing' homelands unleashed ethnic and class forces, which were increasingly difficult for the liberation movements and the black working class to ignore. Of those representative of such forces, Gatsha Buthelezi and his Kwa-Zulu-based Inkhata movement would prove to be the most enduring and vicious. Additionally, although the black middle class was small in relative terms, the new opportunities for its consolidation and growth (along with that of the Indian and Coloured population) provided a stronger petit-bourgeois presence among those opposed to apartheid. While the effects of the reform measures on the growth of a petit-bourgeois class and aspirant black bourgeoisie should not be underestimated, the net result was to widen the faultlines of apartheid capitalism. The other side of the 'total strategy' (that is, militarily opposing what Botha and his securocrats saw as the revolutionary onslaught), was becoming the more attractive option.

Despite the limited military threat of the ANC's armed propaganda efforts, MK did manage to pull off a few spectacular attacks which contributed both to the apartheid state's fears of a revolutionary onslaught and to raising the ANC's symbolic appeal among the masses. Between 1980 and 1982 MK launched mine and rocket attacks on the Sasolburg coal-to-oil refinery, the South African Defence Force's (SADF) Voortrekkerhootge headquarters and the Koeburg nuclear power station in Cape Town. These attacks provided Botha with the excuse to launch his own raids and bombing runs on neighbouring Mozambique and Angola, where MK was now based. Partly to keep his security allies happy and partly to ensure that none of the 'Frontline' states would be able to reduce their economic dependence on their apartheid neighbour, Botha launched a systematic campaign of destabilisation (Hanlon, 1986; Martin and Johnson, 1988).

Using a carrot-and-stick approach – with the emphasis falling on the latter – the apartheid forces waged counter-revolutionary terror. Not content with using its own forces, the apartheid state funded, armed and protected both UNITA and the Mozambican National Resistance (RENAMO) as proxy armies designed to cause maximum damage on the infrastructure of Angola and

Mozambique respectively. The cost borne by these countries was immense. By one account, Mozambique suffered over 1863 closed or destroyed schools by 1987; the national debt (balance of payments) skyrocketed to US$3.4 billion by 1987 (from being virtually zero in 1980); and by the late 1980s an estimated 500,000 people had been killed and over six million displaced (Martin and Johnson, 1988, pp. 1–55). Even if they could not succeed in overthrowing the governments of these two countries, Botha and his cronies made sure they would never be able to sustain an alternative economic and political vision.

The apartheid offensive was, of course, also directed at taking away the capacity of the ANC to carry forward its armed struggle. Mozambique had been the only secure base from which MK could directly infiltrate South Africa, and what successes MK had managed were in no small part due to the use of Mozambique as a forward base of operations. All that changed when Mozambique signed the Nkomati Accord with South Africa in 1984. This stated that, in return for barring MK from its soil, Mozambique would receive Botha's assurance that South Africa would end its support of RENAMO. The Accord proved to be a chimera. MK lost its forward base, but RENAMO was kept well-supplied by the clandestine efforts of the apartheid military. Combining this regional destabilisation with increasingly frequent displays of internal repression – including the introduction of death squads (Laurence, 1990; Pauw, 1991) – Botha had much more success on the repression than the reform front.

As a result of the destabilisation of the Frontline states the ANC became increasingly paralysed organisationally and, as a result, more authoritarian. Often too busy with international diplomatic commitments and at the same time trying to cope with the apartheid state's counter-revolutionary campaign, the leadership lost touch with what was going on inside its own organisation. Its leadership became increasingly paranoid, seeing an apartheid agent hidden in every corner of its security department, and Mbokodo ('the stone that crushes'), began to arrest and interrogate suspected cadres. The latter included extremely harsh techniques, and interrogations were carried out at newly established detention camps/centres.[5] The effects were particularly acute within MK. While the leadership continued to make administrative adjustments (a new Political-Military Council was formed to oversee the armed struggle) and issue new plans for a people's war, large numbers of MK rank and file became increasingly demoralised.

The vast majority of MK recruits were in Angolan camps where many of them had lived for years since fleeing South Africa. Living under difficult conditions, unable to fight inside their own country and increasingly engaged in major battles on the side of the MPLA against UNITA, a growing number of MK cadres began openly to criticise and challenge the leadership. These developments eventually resulted in a series of mutinies within the Angolan camps in which there was armed confrontation between 'loyalist' and smaller 'dissident' MK forces, followed by the detention of most of the mutineers (Ellis and Sechaba, 1992).[6] As an indication of how out of touch much of the leadership had become, Ellis and Sechaba claim that the top ANC leaders were holding a meeting in Luanda to discuss another Joe Slovo paper on extending the 'people's war' at the time when the mutineers were demanding that they be sent back to South Africa to fight (1992, p. 132). In such an environment it was not surprising that many in the ANC leadership wanted to concentrate their efforts in the broader international arena, where events seemed to be less troublesome.

Misdirected Internationalism

The onset of structural crisis in South Africa during the 1970s had alerted leading sections of international and domestic capital to the fact that changes were needed if the possibility of a radical anti-capitalist revolution was to be avoided. To this end one of the major capitalist philanthropic institutions in the United States, the Rockefeller Foundation, funded a study in 1981 entitled *South Africa: Time is Running Out*. This report made several recommendations. These included that the United States should push for genuine power-sharing in South Africa; that assistance should be given for the economic development of southern Africa to reduce its dependence on apartheid South Africa; that the arms embargo against South Africa should be expanded; and that American companies should halt new investment. Even though the report was not endorsed by all sections of international capital, it exemplified a definite shift in perspective. The ANC could not have put forward a better argument for international involvement in its anti-apartheid struggle.

Not long after the publication of the Rockefeller report, Oliver Tambo met representatives of leading American corporations and banks (Karis, 1983, p. 195). At the meeting, he gave assurances that their presence in a post-apartheid state would be welcome – subject to new regulations that an ANC government would institute (*New York Times*, 7 February 1982). Although this meeting probably represented no more than a sounding-out session, it was important for other reasons: it confirmed a long-standing strategic principle that had become obscured by all the harsh Cold War rhetoric and violence – that the ANC was not averse to dealing with anyone who could be a potential anti-apartheid ally.

On the other side of the coin, international capital (represented in this case by leading American capitalists) was belatedly acknowledging the importance of the ANC to any future economic and political South African formation. This was confirmed by Robert McNamara, who had recently retired as President of the World Bank (and was a former US Secretary of Defense) in a speech delivered at the University of the Witswatersrand in Johannesburg on 21 October 1982. He argued that US policy should be 'based on the recognition that black nationalism in South Africa is a struggle whose eventual success can at most be delayed – and at immense cost – but not permanently denied' (*The Times*, 22 October 1982). Such conclusions were not limited to the Americans. British capital, with its historic involvement in the South African economy, also grasped the necessity of dealing with the ANC – its anti-liberation rhetoric aside. According to one leading ANC member, Oliver Tambo met representatives of British banks and corporations several times in the early 1980s (Turok, personal interview, October 1992).

Although these meetings were consistent with the ANC's international campaign to isolate the apartheid state, their importance lies in the way the two sides strategically conceptualised their respective agendas. The ANC was all too ready to enlist the anti-apartheid support of the international community in its broad national democratic revolution without a corresponding analysis, reflected in practice, of the specific strategic agenda of certain international actors.

For the core Western capitalist states (the United States, Britain, France and Germany) and representatives of international capital, such a political and economic agenda reflected their own strategic national and/or material interests. This agenda, while adaptable to changing international conditions, consisted of a fundamental commitment to implementing:

- a process of accumulation through the exploitation (in varied forms) of human and natural resources in the third world;
- using various military and financial resources and institutions to influence the struggle for, and exercise of, political and economic power in the third world;
- enforcing the adoption of a free-market capitalist ideology and practice through these same resources and institutions;
- creating new, and/or support existing, social and political forces that would be in direct opposition to any revolutionary organisation or activity which might fundamentally threaten these interests.

As we shall see, the ANC's failure to incorporate a serious analysis of this agenda into its practical strategy was to have a profound impact on the willingness and ability of the ANC to achieve the goal of transformative liberation. As it stood, the ANC was content to adopt the tactic of talking to its different constituencies with different voices.

In its international campaign for the isolation of the apartheid state, the ANC's argument that international capital should disinvest found increasing resonance with corporate and finance capital (McKinley, 1986). The majority of the anti-apartheid movements in Europe and the United States backed the ANC's call for disinvestment on moral grounds, and generated active public pressure on investors in South Africa to desist from aiding the apartheid regime. However, in the early stages of disinvestment the main impetus for capital was not moral but rather hard-nosed capitalist considerations. As one informed commentator argued in 1983: 'Internal political risk studies rather than protests of pressure groups have influenced bank decisions about loans to South Africa' (Pomeroy, 1986, p. 152). Whatever the motivations, the ANC saw the gathering campaign as a confirmation that the 'international pillar' of its struggle was succeeding.

The ANC was not unaware that the actions of certain Western governments were designed to push for an accommodationist solution to apartheid. A prime example was the US administration's policy of constructive engagement. As argued by its main proponent, Under-Secretary for African Affairs Chester Crocker, constructive engagement stressed the need for close cooperation with the apartheid state in the hope of persuading it to introduce democracy. Similarly, the policy sought to put pressure on the national liberation movements to accept an 'evolutionary, non-violent' process of democratisation (Crocker, 1980/81, pp. 323–57). The 'constructive' methods chosen – diplomatic, material and indirect military support to the apartheid state – made it quite clear to the ANC that the goal of such a policy was a deracialised capitalism in which strategic Western interests would be guaranteed. The ANC thus issued scathing attacks, as exemplified by the following ANC NEC statement of 8 January 1983:

> Its [the United States] support for the apartheid regime consists precisely in encouraging these fascists to intensify their counter-offensive and in guaranteeing them immunity from punitive international action. Every crime that the Pretoria regime commits, be it in South Africa, Namibia or elsewhere, bears Washington's stamp of approval. This regime goes into action backed by the logistic, financial, and political support of the United States. The apartheid regime, acting in its own right and in the furtherance of the global strategy of the United States, constitutes a strikeforce for the accomplishment of the counter-

revolutionary objective of defeating the progressive forces of Southern Africa, including SWAPO and the ANC, and transforming our region into an exclusive economic, political, and military preserve of the imperialist world. (ANC, 1983b)

What the ANC seemed unable to grasp was that the ultimate strategic goal of both (friendly and unfriendly) international capital and Western governments, such as the United States and Britain, was a deracialised capitalism. The different tactics used to help achieve such a goal were mirrored in capital and the governments' respective world-views and what was perceived as satisfying immediate short-term interests.

Such complementary goals do not imply that a conspiracy emanated from the bowels of corporate headquarters and government buildings in the West. It is merely the recognition of the specific and complex strategy and tactics of political and economic representatives of capital. The South African 'question' was not the sole possession of the ANC and the apartheid state, and their respective strategies and tactics were certainly not competing in an international vacuum. While garnering international support should be one of the essential tasks of any liberation movement, it was the way in which the ANC set out to achieve this that raises serious questions about its strategy for genuine national liberation. By extending its 'united front' approach to the international arena, the ANC was extending open invitations to a host of incredibly powerful forces to play potentially important roles in influencing the direction and character of the South African liberation struggle. The implications of this will be developed in the next chapter, but suffice to say that by the mid-1980s the ANC had begun to build upon the already existing foundation of an international politics of accommodation.

Internal Mobilisation

While the ANC and the apartheid state were devoting large amounts of energy and time to regional and international work, the internal situation was hotting up. Botha's attempts at reform had made little headway in achieving the government's main goal of coopting large numbers of the non-white population. A good example was the formation of the Tricameral Parliament in May 1983. Designed to bring Coloureds and Indians into the political 'mainstream', it was only the Botha government that was surprised when the subsequent election was boycotted by the vast majority of both Coloured and Indian people.

The apartheid state was also unwilling to carry out the necessary political reform that might have received favourable responses from the majority of the population and the ANC; and the deep structural economic crisis made it impossible for Botha and the regime to buy its way out. At the same time that he had introduced the Tricameral Parliament, Botha had also introduced provisions granting the President wide-sweeping executive powers. Instead of the quiescence desired, increasing numbers of workers, students and unemployed intensified their economic and political demands. Most of the issues central to these demands were focused on local grassroots economic and social conditions (wages, education, housing, rent, electricity) and political involvement (municipal council representation, policing). These demands, and the need to organise around them, led to the phenomenal growth of civic associations and community organisations formed around varying social sectors (students, women, religion, trade unions, ethnicity).

The desire to bring together these disparate struggles on a national level in order to combat Botha's powers and reforms led to the formation of the National Forum in June 1983. Representatives of AZAPO, the Cape Action League and a few ANC-aligned activists were all present at its opening conference. Shunning the 'charterist' tradition (so-called after the adoption of the Freedom Charter) as too liberal and ethnically defined, the National Forum adopted an 'Azanian Manifesto' which called for an anti-racialist struggle against capitalism and apartheid. However, although its criticisms of the charterists may be deemed accurate, the National Forum exhibited an ignorance of strategic organising. The Forum, which itself was riddled with ideological disunity, placed far too much emphasis on the power of ideology as a mobilising tool. As a result, it severely limited its scope of influence, effectively cut itself off from the grassroots and compromised its ability to act as a militant unifier. Whatever chance the Forum had of sharing a common platform with the charterists was quickly struck down by the externalised ANC NEC. In a statement sounding very much like the work of Stalinist ideologues, the NEC denounced

> those who, while posing as socialists ... and defenders of Black pride, seek to divide the people and divert them from the pursuit of the goals enshrined in the Freedom Charter. Through their activities, these elements show hatred for the Charter and mass united action, no less virulent than that displayed by the Pretoria regime. (A. Marx, 1992, p. 120)

The charterists quickly disassociated themselves from the Forum and undertook efforts to launch their own national organisation.

These efforts eventually led to the formation of the United Democratic Front (UDF) in August 1983. Conceived of as an umbrella organisation of all 'progressive' people and groupings, the UDF consisted of groups and individuals from every imaginable sector of South African society. Although the UDF did not openly align itself with any political formation, it was obvious from its inception that the UDF reflected the same strategic approach as the ANC. The UDF's initial 1983 declaration declared that:

> we, the freedom loving people of South Africa, say with one voice to the whole world that we,
> - cherish the vision of a united, democratic South Africa based on the will of the people,
> - will strive for the unity of all people through united action against the evils of apartheid, economic, and all other forms of exploitation.
>
> And, in our march to a free and just South Africa, we are guided by these noble ideals
> - we stand for the creation of a true democracy in which all South Africans will participate in the government of our country;
> - we stand for a single non-racial, unfragmented South Africa. (UDF, 1993)

If the National Forum had put too much emphasis on ideology, the UDF attempted to make it almost non-existent. Stressing the strategic primacy of the unity of all South Africans and welcoming anyone who opposed apartheid into its ranks – although it helped if one was a charterist – the UDF consciously sought to project a non-ideological image. Much like the ANC, the UDF leadership argued that national unity required the blurring of class divisions and the adoption of the broadest possible programme of inclusiveness. Such an approach was reflected in the make-up of the UDF, whose ranks included organisations ranging from the all-white, all-female and decidedly upper-middle class Black Sash (a national, liberal advocacy group), to radical and predominantly working-class organisations such as the Tumahole Youth Congress (a civic group based in the Free State province). By avoiding potentially divisive ideological formulations, the UDF succeeded in bringing together the largest and most socially heterogeneous organisation yet seen in South Africa.

Although this strategic approach was partly explained by the UDF's desire to operate legally, in reality it reflected a specific ideological choice. The UDF's claims of purely strategic considerations over those of ideology were specious. Ideology, of whatever stripe, informs strategy and to claim that one has no ideology is in itself an ideological choice. In other words, the UDF was using a particular ideological approach to conceptualise the 'nation' and opposition to those it considered outside of this. That it happened to be an approach which stressed social/class inclusiveness made it no less ideological.

Some analysts have contrasted the ideological inclinations of groups such as the National Forum and the non-ideological inclinations of the UDF (Lodge and Nasson, 1991; Lodge, 1985). This is both analytically wrong and misdirected. Such an analysis assumes that ideology (most often defined as a coherent set of values/beliefs) is the exclusive preserve of those on the left or the right of the political and social spectrum, where those who steer a 'middle course' (whatever label one wants to give them) are then seen as having no specific ideology. Such 'centrism', which most often seeks to find commonalities among division, is itself constitutive of an ideology. It is no less a coherent set of beliefs that informs strategic decisions than any other -ism. The fact that such 'centrism' borrows from other ideological constructs does not make it an atomised collection of disparate influences.

While UDF membership was spread across a broad social and class spectrum, the national leadership consisted mainly of a middle-class intelligentsia, most of whom were ANC stalwarts or recently converted charterists (former BCM adherents). These included leaders such as Allan Boesak, Frank Chikane (church-affiliated), Mewa Ramgobin (Indian activist), Albertina Sisulu, Archie Gumede, Murphy Morobe and Patrick 'Terror' Lekota (all civic/township association activists). Throughout the first year of its existence the UDF conducted high-profile campaigns against the Botha reform agenda. In its bid to create as broad a united front as possible, the UDF began to woo white and black capitalists – a move that brought the UDF financial assistance and a constituency whose conceptualisation of national liberation (as a means of getting a bigger and better slice of the pie) stretched its meaning to breaking point.

Many major (white) South African capitalists were only too happy to provide financial assistance to the UDF (for example, Chris Ball, the South African head of British-based Barclays Bank). As previously mentioned, domestic capital had long realised that to save its cherished free enterprise system it would have to find ways to influence the 'struggle'. As long as domestic capital was certain that the UDF, and later the ANC, were open to the vision of a deracialised capitalism, it knew it would be much better off nailing its colours to the national democratic mast.

With the full backing of the externalised ANC, the UDF launched its internal struggle. One of its first national campaigns focused on the demand for the release of Mandela. This campaign signalled the beginning of what became the idolisation of Nelson Mandela as the embodiment of the liberation struggle (ANC, 1983a). More generally though, the UDF provided the ANC with an ally whose strategic approach was consistent with its own, an internal base within which it could now popularise its national democratic message, and a mast on which to fly the internal flag of the ANC. Indeed, the ANC was eager to counter the perception that the organisation was 'a transient force having it's [sic] roots on foreign soil and drawing it's [sic] main support from forces outside our borders' (ANC, 1984b, p. 9).

Despite organisational problems and the blows inflicted by the apartheid state's regional destabilisation, internal developments (and the international campaigns) shone as a beacon of hope for the future internal struggle of the ANC. These developments were positive enough to encourage the ANC's NEC to increase talk about the seizure of power. Ironically, on the day that the Nkomati Accord was signed, which robbed MK of its most important frontline base, the ANC confidently declared:

> The central and immediate question of South African politics is the overthrow of the white minority regime, the seizure of power and the uprooting ... of the entire apartheid system of colonial and racist domination, fascist tyranny, the super-exploitation of the black majority, and imperialist aggression and expansionism. The question will be and is being settled, in struggle, within the borders of our country and nowhere else. (ANC, 1984a)

Many inside South Africa were to take this statement very seriously.

4

The Politics of Ungovernability: Insurrectionary Hopes and Strategic Realities (1985–89)

> we call on all sections of our people to make the apartheid system more and more unworkable and the country less and less governable. At the same time we must work endlessly to strengthen all levels of mass and underground organisation and to create the beginnings of popular power.
>
> ANC NEC Statement[1]

The internal mass struggles in South Africa during the mid-1980s were a direct result of the politicisation of domestic material and social grievances. This process was helped by the ANC's tactical calls for ungovernability and the prosecution of a 'people's war'. However, the strategic realities of realising the seizure of power demanded that armed mass struggle be centred on internal working-class-led organisation. Unfortunately for the masses, the macro-strategy of both the externalised ANC and the internal UDF did not provide the necessary foundation.

As a result, the internal struggles took place with little organisational basis, direction or discipline, and this led to much of their revolutionary potential being squandered: ungovernability became 'unguided missile' politics. The practical results of such a politics – organisational division, semi-anarchy, increased vulnerability to enemy infiltration and attack – in turn led straight back to an externally dominated liberatory thrust, which further entrenched a politics of accommodation.

Uprising from Below

As had been the case so many times in the history of South Africa's liberation struggle, the initial spark for (yet another) uprising came from below. The UDF's first national campaigns, aimed at exposing the Tricameral Parliament as an apartheid sham and opposing Botha's abrogation of executive powers, spurred the growth of new grassroots organisations. However, these campaigns did not directly address the deteriorating material and social conditions which apartheid capitalism continued to engender. People on the ground seemed determined to launch their own frontal assault. On 3 September 1984, the day of the installation of Botha's Tricameral Parliament, the townships in the Vaal triangle[2] near Johannesburg erupted. No longer willing to tolerate local apartheid controls and feeling the full brunt of the economic crisis, residents took to the streets, burning businesses and government buildings, setting up roadblocks, fighting the police and attacking municipal councillors. So began the most intense and sustained mass struggle in the history of South Africa.

What made the Vaal uprising so significant was the linkage that the residents made between local grievances and national political and economic change. Unlike much of the earlier mass struggle, this uprising did not emanate from a national leadership intent on realising specifically formulated political goals, but was the direct expression of grassroots politicisation. No longer prepared to tolerate rent hikes, exploitative labour conditions, appalling living conditions, inadequate education and corrupt, state-appointed local councillors, the Vaal residents directed their anger at anything representative of apartheid capitalism.

The knock-on effect of the Vaal uprising was impressive in its breadth and speed and it caught all the major players (ANC, SACP, UDF and the apartheid state) by surprise. Within weeks of the first street battles in the Vaal triangle several areas of the country were literally ablaze. Besides the industrial belt around Johannesburg there was intense activity in the Eastern and Western Cape regions and to a lesser extent in the Northern Transvaal. Most of the civic associations and other groups which took up the struggle quickly affiliated to the UDF (if they did not already belong to it), but there were also active groups affiliated to the BCM tradition, such as the Azanian Students Movement.

A brief overview of events during late 1984 and early 1985 testifies to the extent and depth of the uprising:

- A call in November for a two-day general strike in the Transvaal, orchestrated by the Federation of South African Trade Unions and the Soweto Youth Congress was heeded by over a million workers (which included migrant hostel dwellers).
- A stay-away called by the Port Elizabeth Black Civic Association (PEBCO) was backed by 90 per cent of workers in the city (Lodge and Nasson, 1991, p. 73).
- The Cradock Residents' Association and its leader Matthew Goniwe succeeded in building a network of civic and youth organisations across the rural Eastern Cape during the months following the Vaal uprising, which effectively replaced apartheid authority in the respective black townships.

Besides the more organised resistance, thousands of youth engaged in pitched battles with police, often without any formal leadership or structure. Many were responding directly to the ANC's well-publicised call in early 1985 to make the townships, and ultimately the country, ungovernable. Tellingly though, neither the ANC nor the UDF was able to exercise much control or direction over the often spontaneous expressions of resistance from the grassroots.

It was partly the implicit anti-capitalist content of the Vaal uprising, and the subsequent nationwide mass struggle, that gave it a historic opportunity for realising a radically transformative politics. A strategy was needed that would build on the people's anger; a strategy that organised and provided leadership to struggles that would be equally undermining to both the institutions and practice of political and economic oppression (that is, apartheid and capitalism). To channel the people's militancy into a narrow framework of anti-apartheidism would mean denying the rich possibilities of that struggle to challenge fundamentally the foundation of people's oppression.

In consideration of the objective conditions already discussed in this study, which included a highly politicised, urbanised and pro-letarianised South African population, a strategy which centred on internal, working-class-led organisation and struggle would potentially provide the strongest challenge to apartheid capitalism. And yet the strategy and tactics of the ANC, while rhetorically strong with regard to the potential leading role of the working class and a full transfer of power to the people, was constitutive of everything that militated against such an approach. Instead, the reality consisted of a strategy and tactics in which the organisational centre of the ANC was externalised; in which thousands of the best activists sat in far-flung military camps waiting to launch (or so they were told) an armed seizure of power; and which was undergirded by an ideological commitment that limited the struggles of the mass base to a racially privileged first stage of national liberation.

In retrospect what the Vaal residents and others engaging in a life-and-death struggle against the combined ravages of apartheid and capitalism needed was proactive revolutionary organisation and leadership. Despite the narrowly conceived strategic approach of the ANC, it was testimony to its (and its allies) political hegemony within the country that most people turned to the ANC, SACP and UDF for organisation and leadership.

The Kabwe Conference

Although commentators often make a direct correlation between the general upsurge in struggle following the Vaal uprising and the

Second ANC Consultative Conference at Kabwe, Zambia (16–23 June 1985), the reasons lay elsewhere.

Following the Angolan camp mutinies there had been intense pressure from the MK rank and file for a full conference of the ANC. The leadership informally agreed to meet this request before the events of late 1984. In addition, top SACP leaders had been pushing for the opening up of the ANC NEC to non-Africans – something that could be decided only at a full organisational conference. The fact that the Kabwe Conference was held amidst the most intense mass struggle period in the history of South Africa presented the ANC with a unique opportunity to formulate a strategy and tactics which would provide the internal resistance with the direction and organisation they required to carry through a revolutionary struggle for liberation. This needed to be the main task if there was going to be any possibility of achieving what the ANC had for so long stated was their goal of struggle: the seizure of power.

A full account of the proceedings of the Kabwe Conference is somewhat clouded and conflicting accounts abound. Some have described it as being dominated by SACP members, riddled by ethnic rivalries and characterised by anti-democratic voting procedures. From these accounts it appears that certain high-ranking officials, in particular MK leaders, exploited ethnic identification (the main divisions being Xhosa/Zulu/Tswana) as a means to pursue their respective power agendas, and that the Stuart Commission Report (so named after James Stuart, a senior movement leader tasked with writing the report) on the Angolan mutinies was never tabled for full discussion (Ellis and Sechaba, 1992, pp. 149–51; Mkatashingo, 1991, pp. 91–2). Other accounts paint of a picture of a democratically rejuvenated ANC, more responsive than ever to its rank and file and less susceptible to negative external influences (Lodge, 1985, pp. 89–90).

The first full conference since Morogoro, Kabwe was meant to give voice to those of the 1976 generation who now made up the majority of the externalised organisation. Whatever account of the conference is cited it seems that the established ANC and SACP leadership and long-serving ANC officials dominated the proceedings – one of the more contentious practices allowed at Kabwe was giving ex-officio officials the right to vote as delegates. By all accounts much debate was taken up with the issue of NEC open membership, and despite some spirited opposition the motion was passed. ANC President-General Tambo presented a list of candidates for the NEC (now expanded to 30 members) as a guide to selection – as it turned out all members of the new NEC came from the list. Among others, these included SACP heavyweights Joe Slovo, Mac Maharaj and James Stuart.

On strategic matters the conference reaffirmed the Freedom Charter as the 'ideological lodestar' of the ANC, rejected the idea of a negotiated settlement with the apartheid state and confirmed the shift to a people's war strategy. Following previous SACP formulations closely (the SACP had held its own Congress in Moscow in December 1984), the conference asserted that 'victory' could come only through the 'seizure of power' (Lodge, 1985, p. 82). While this position was consistent with past ANC strategic formulations, it was no doubt given added impetus by the Vaal uprising and the subsequent intensity of the internal struggle. The only difference was that a seizure of power would now come about through the prosecution of a people's war as opposed to a protracted and predominantly rural-based guerrilla war. In the words of the SACP:

> Our situation displays almost all the conditions for a violent revolution that does not have to mature from a guerrilla campaign ... our conduct of people's war has to take into account ... the ongoing uprisings which have elements of an insurrectionary revolt ... insurrection is much more than a possibility at the very end of a protracted war. We have to merge the strategy of protracted war and the science and art of insurrection. (SACP, 1986a, p. 3)

The debate over the prosecution of a people's war had been taking place within ANC and SACP intellectual circles since the early 1980s. However, with the onset of the internal uprising it was now married to the idea of insurrection. The idea of a people's war was premised on a strategic approach which sought to use the movement's armed forces (MK) and key internal activists to act as scholars/soldiers in rural and urban communities as the best way to mobilise and activate the masses. Instead of seeking to conduct classic guerrilla warfare by engaging the enemy, the movement's cadres would now seek to arm and train people in their communities. This strategy was intended to give people the means to launch effective armed and mass resistance to the apartheid state – a process which it was hoped would culminate in an insurrectionary seizure of power. As will be discussed in later chapters the potential success of such a strategy rested on the degree to which the movement's cadres could build and sustain solid internal organisational structures. Such a goal had been asserted as central to previous ANC strategy, but had rarely developed past conference resolutions and ANC NEC statements.

The argument that the prevailing objective conditions inside South Africa and in the southern African region proved an insurmountable barrier to building an effective internal underground cannot wholly account for the ANC's consistent failure, since

1963, to do so. The ANC's strategic approach to the liberation struggle had also precluded the building of such internal structures. Although this goal was repeated time and again in ANC statements and publications, the practice which subsequently followed, emanating and directed as it was from an external base, had the effect of appending the internal dynamic. By doing so, the ANC undercut substantially the possibility of ever achieving the one element central to a successful seizure of power – an armed, mass-based internal cadre.

The immediate rejection of a negotiated settlement at Kabwe went hand-in-hand with the call for an insurrectionary people's war, just as it had when the best vehicle for liberation was viewed as being protracted guerrilla warfare. In the quasi-insurrectionary climate gripping the country as well as the ANC, it would have been virtually impossible for the organisation to endorse moves towards a negotiated settlement. In this regard the Kabwe decision represented a continuity with past pronouncements.

The debate on the new approach to the prosecution of the war effort was concluded with the revamping of the Politico-Military Council which was given the task of setting up Regional Politico-Military Councils (RPMCs – to be set up in all the major areas of operation) in order to implement the move towards a people's war. However, the committee which was set up to revise the Kabwe report on strategy and tactics had not completed its work by early 1989, nor is there any official record of it ever completing its work (Barrell, 1990, p. 59) – confirmation of the yawning gap between the ANC's stated intentions and its practice. One leading ANC member has gone so far as to say that the Kabwe call for an insur-rectionary seizure of power 'was nonsense' and that the armed struggle, in whatever form, was always seen by the leadership as 'a half-hearted thing' (Turok, personal interview, October 1992). As SACP Central Committee and ANC NEC member Jeremy Cronin has pointed out, there was a tendency to be 'dogmatic about our slogans', something he blames on 'bad external habits' (personal interview, October 1992).

After 24 years, the armed struggle was as far from seizing power as the movement leadership was from Johannesburg. The practical history and character of the ANC's leadership, combined with the structural barriers to the chosen strategy of liberation, make it extremely difficult to argue that this leadership wholly believed in what they were telling the movement's cadres and the masses. In this regard, the Kabwe Conference, above all, represented another missed opportunity. The combination of organisational and ideological power-plays, and the evident triumph of radical rhetoric over practical strategic implementation, affected the ability and capacity of the ANC, through the rank and file, to implement a strategy conducive to creating the opportunities for a radically transformative national liberation.

The Struggle for People's Power

By the middle of 1985, while the ANC was consulting at Kabwe, the UDF leadership was trying to catch up. It admitted as much in its 1985 National General Council Report, which stated: 'In many areas, organisations trail behind the masses, thus making it more difficult for a disciplined mass action to take place' (Lodge and Nasson, 1991, p. 76).

The ANC and UDF were not the only ones who found it difficult to cope with militant resistance. Vacillating between harsh repression and the introduction of further reform, the apartheid state found itself in temporary disarray. For the first few months of the uprising the Botha government allowed the continued legal operation of the UDF and its affiliates, hoping that the resistance would burn itself out and that an increasing number of township dwellers would respond to its (generally unpopular) attempts at cooption. However, with the uprising showing no signs of abating, a partial state of emergency was declared on 21 July. At the same time apartheid security forces were given wide powers of arrest, detention and search and seizure.

One of the first victims was the UDF's largest affiliate: the Congress of South African Students (COSAS) was banned and many of its leaders arrested. In an attempt to stamp out grassroots resistance and organisation this was followed by the arrest and detention of many of the UDF's regional and national leadership, as well a show of force in the townships. Despite these measures, the apartheid state failed to crush grassroots opposition. People were bloodied, but certainly not bowed. The apartheid state's vision of a pacified black populace was met with a rude introduction to the reality of militant black resistance.

While the police and youth fought it out on the streets, the UDF began to encourage a change of tactics in an attempt to exert more control over local struggles. Arguing that there was a need to hit the apartheid state economically, UDF leaders called for consumer boycotts against local white businesses. Although nationwide boycotts ensued, the tactic met with varying degrees of success, with the major campaigns concentrated in the cities of Port Elizabeth and East London and around the Witswatersrand region. Unfortunately many of these actions were marked by coercion, criminal elements acting in the name of the UDF/ANC/SACP and the development of an intolerance for those who advocated different tactics. This highlighted a major inadequacy of those who were ostensibly leading the mass struggle. Without well-organised, popular underground structures able to give direction, disciplined leadership and effective armed support for legitimate resistance, much of the potential for realising the stated goals of the uprising was squandered.

As in the past, the organised black working class was the leading element in the liberation struggle. Coming together in the newly formed Congress of South African Trade Unions (COSATU) in November 1985, the working class was able to take its economic muscle directly into the political arena.

COSATU brought together unions that had been in FOSATU, several independent unions and the huge National Union of Mineworkers (NUM), formerly affiliated to CUSA. By doing so, much of the division that had been part of the charterist-workerist debate was temporarily closed. Linking up with community and student groups and bringing with it the militancy of hundreds of thousands of workers, COSATU provided much-needed cohesion and direction to the continuing resistance. Not long after its formation COSATU leaders travelled to Lusaka to meet with the externalised ANC and SACP leadership. They subsequently endorsed the Freedom Charter and allied COSATU to both organisations.

These developments were indicative of the dominant ideological and symbolic appeal of the ANC and the SACP, as well as the growing politicisation of the new union structures. None the less, there was still a great deal of antipathy among many workers and worker leaders towards the SACP and their two-stage national democratic revolution strategy. Some saw the SACP as having questionable democratic credentials; its formulations as diluting specific working-class concerns in its alliance with the ANC and of placing the struggle for socialism on the back burner. The SACP itself continued to argue that 'workerism' was necessarily 'reformist' and lashed out at 'workerists' who mooted the idea of forming a specifically workers' party as not dedicated to the 'overthrow of capitalism' (SACP, 1986, p. 7).

Although COSATU provided working-class discipline and organisational direction to ongoing resistance (for example, the 1987 miners' strike), its alliance with the ANC/SACP/UDF meant that its efforts were bound up in the overall strategic path that was now dominated by a politics of ungovernability. This was a negative development. It was not that a struggle to make the system ungovernable was in itself negative; it was rather that the underlying liberation strategy of the ANC made a politics of ungovernability (under the structural conditions present) an unguided missile politics – that is, one of little cohesion, specific strategic direction or with a grounded base.

Despite these strategic shortcomings, the intensity of grassroots struggle continued well into 1986. The ANC and its UDF internal allies were riding high on the wave of ungovernability. With the added strength of COSATU an attitude of supreme confidence reigned that liberation, or as the nationwide slogan proclaimed, 'people's power', was just around the corner. Since the general uprising had taken hold, the notion of people's power had surfaced as the defining goal of resistance, to be achieved in conjunction with the prosecution of a people's war: a people's war would provide the organisational and military means to achieve people's power. The degree to which the confidence of movement strategists informed the extent of people's power is exemplified by the following definition:

> Control over every aspect of our lives – at work; at school; where we live; over the structures of national and local government; over the army, police, courts, and prisons; the media; the church; financial institutions and the economy as a whole. (Morris, undated, p. 108)

The belief that the apartheid state was on the brink of collapse and to be replaced by organs of people's power was promulgated by leaders and taken up by the masses. UDF leader Mohammed Valli confidently declared in March 1986 that the UDF could withstand 'extreme repression' and 'dictate the nature and pace of events in our country' (*Weekly Mail*, 14 March 1986). In a widely reported speech which exhibited a more crude version of the confidence that gripped township youths, Winnie Mandela (wife of Nelson Mandela and by now a national and international political figure) confidently declared that the liberation of South Africa would be gained through the use of 'necklaces' and 'little boxes of matches'.[3] In the townships and some rural areas slogans such as 'liberation before education' and 'people's justice' clearly expressed the belief among many people at the grassroots, in particular the youth, that they were well on the way to overthrowing the apartheid state.

The notion of people's power and the idea that dual power (parallel institutions controlled by the masses) was on the verge of delivering national liberation, confused hope with reality. Although resistance had certainly made substantial inroads into the apartheid state's control of the townships and to a lesser degree in some of the rural areas, the national authority and coercive capacity of the apartheid state was nowhere near being threatened with disintegration. The key ingredients for a potentially insurrection-ist seizure of power in the South African context – strategically organised, armed and nationally consolidated organs of people's power – were absent. As it stood, the apartheid state, although facing a serious economic crisis and a political crisis of legitimacy, was not fundamentally undermined.

This does not imply that the activities of the numerous civic organisations (especially those based in urban townships), undertaken as they were within the context of the ANC's call for ungovernability, had no substantive impact. As a former President of the Alexandra Civic Organisation has argued, the most important contribution of this period of struggle was the growing confidence among the people that they had to 'be involved in making their own future' (Mayekiso, 1993, pp. 24–7). While the possibility of an insurrectionary seizure of power was fundamentally undermined by the strategic vision and practice of an externalised liberation movement, local struggles did lay the foundation for the potential extension of grassroots empowerment and a vision of transformation centred on a materially located struggle.

The Bitter Fruits of Apartheid's 'Total Strategy'

The euphoria that had gripped liberation movement leaders and their followers after the lifting of the first state of emergency in early March 1986 was short-lived. Only three months later, on 12 June, P.W. Botha announced a nationwide state of emergency which gave virtual control of the country to the securocrats in his cabinet. Flushed with their successful destabilisation activities in the region (for example, in Mozambique), the securocrats were given free rein to implement their own version of a total (counter-revolutionary) strategy. The securocrats, concentrated in the professional ranks of the SADF and generally seeing the police force as ill-educated and crude operators, believed that their more sophisticated counter-revolutionary tactics (centred on waging low-intensity warfare) would be better able to maintain law and order while defusing the uprising.

Within weeks of the state of emergency, the securocrats had deployed thousands of SADF troops into the townships, had drastically increased arrests and detentions, and had instituted harsh censorship regulations on the press. Operating within a militarised National Security Management System which created a web of regional and sub-regional security committees, and with an executive-controlled State Security Council providing political muscle, the securocrats set about implementing their counter-revolutionary strategy. As part of this strategy they sought to prioritise security considerations as a means to open space for further reform measures – for example, by using extreme force and terror to break the revolutionary spirit of the opposition and thus create opportunities for cooption. This approach reversed the previous situation where failed reforms had been followed by more limited repression. In order to create the maximum space for the success of this strategy several new tactics were adopted. These included plans to:

- decapitate the national and local leadership of the ANC/SACP/UDF through mass arrest, indefinite detention and where deemed necessary, through assassination and murder. Successful regional counter-revolutionary efforts would continue;
- provide organised resistance to the ANC/SACP/UDF in the townships along ethnic, class and ideological lines as well as to recruit and/or coopt sections of the black populace to act as vigilante enforcers of the status quo;
- win the hearts and minds of the black population by emphasising selective redistribution of social services and increased opportunities for social advancement, albeit within the parameters of macro-apartheid.

By the end of the year several thousand people had been arrested, the majority of whom were community activists and students; many were children barely out of their teens. Battles raged in numerous townships and in the rural areas of Natal, not only between apartheid security forces and ANC-aligned supporters, but increasingly between these supporters and other blacks representing state-sponsored vigilantism and competing political groups such as Inkhata. In the case of Inkhata and its leader, Gatsha Buthelezi, the state was able to manipulate conflict by turning Inkhata into an ethnically based surrogate which ostensibly sought to combat the 'communism' of the ANC Alliance and preserve Zulu 'culture' through appeals to rural-based Zulu identity.

In response, and as part of yet another attempt to marshall its disorganised forces and give national direction to a situation that verged on anarchy, the UDF launched two nationwide campaigns in late 1986 and early 1987. Yet both the 'Christmas Against the Emergency Campaign' and the 'Unban the ANC' campaign (with full-page newspaper advertisements costing tens of thousands of rands) met with limited organisational success and certainly did little to turn the tide that was now running heavily against the two-year uprising. As one observer noted at the time, 'the UDF's reliance on mobilization and protest often conflicts with organisational requirements. Resources which could be devoted to organization have been dissipated in attempts to mobilize dramatic ... campaigns' (Friedman, 1987, p. 63). The UDF was having great difficulty living up to the earlier claims of its leaders.

As the total strategy of the securocrats took its physical and psychological toll, serious divisions within resistance circles and in the black urban population began to appear. Many township residents were increasingly alienated by the enforcement of boycotts and the often indiscriminate use of people's justice by township youth, commonly referred to as 'comtsotsis',[4] acting in the name of the ANC/SACP/UDF. Likewise, many union members expressed their opposition to the mobilisation strategies of many UDF activists and the increasingly authoritarian practices used to ensure their success. Even voicing these criticisms was often seen as a betrayal of the symbols of the struggle. As one COSATU member said, 'they say you are against Mandela and nobody wants to be accused of that' (Friedman, 1987, p. 67).

There were also battles between national UDF affiliates such as the National Education Coordinating Committee (NECC) and local student bodies over the efficacy of continuing school boycotts. One other example of growing intolerance and division was the internecine battles waged between UDF supporters and those affiliated to AZAPO. Increasingly, UDF leaders sought to project a unified opposition under the charterist banner, giving at least indirect support to the activities of their youthful firebrands. Although many leaders in the UDF argued that the apartheid state's counter-revolutionary strategies were to blame for these divisions, there was a tendency to underplay the responsibility of the UDF's strategies themselves.

Just when the need for building an effective underground to cope with the increased repression and providing organisation and direction to grassroots struggles was greatest, the UDF responded by restructuring its national bureaucracy and embarking on a campaign to win the hearts and minds of the white populace and liberal domestic capital. Campaigns such as the 'Friends of the UDF' launched at one of Johannesburg's plushest hotels followed, and conferences with white liberal organisations such as veteran opposition politician Frederick Van Zyl Slabbert's Institute for Democratic Alternatives in South Africa – IDASA (Lodge, 1987, p. 6) were organised. The UDF leadership had certainly changed its tune since its 1985 assessment of Van Zyl Slabbert (a leading member of the Progressive Federal Party), when he had made calls for negotiation. In the first issue of the UDF's journal *Isizwe* (The Nation), the leadership had declared that Van Zyl Slabbert's attempts at seeking 'closed-door talks' were only 'another attempt to keep the broad mass of South Africans off the political stage'. It went on to say that if there was any lesson to be learned, it was that 'you cannot negotiate "reforms" over the heads of the people' (UDF, 1985, pp. 20–1).

While Van Zyl Slabbert and other political representatives of domestic capital might have been more willing to accept the legitimacy of the UDF, and by association the ANC, than in 1985, the fact that the UDF leadership was now focusing substantial attention and organisational energy on wooing white capital and political liberals bore testimony to the defeat of any genuine notion of an insurrectionary implementation of people's power. The UDF's stated tactics in dealing with domestic capital were designed to 'maintain the division' between 'sections of capital and the National Party' so as to 'neutralise sections of the enemy camp or its allies and thus dislocate their attempts at unity' (UDF, 1985, p. 15). This was directly in line with the ANC tactic of isolating the apartheid regime by bringing together the broadest anti-apartheid front possible. This tactic is discussed more fully in the next chapter, but, it is worth pointing out here that such an approach, by narrowly following the two-stage theory of revolution, allowed for a conceptual division between apartheid and capitalism. The result of this tactic was to lead to a strategic alliance with important sections of capital against the apartheid state.

Indeed, the question arises as to the strategic conceptualisation of the resistance by certain UDF leaders from the very beginning. UDF co-president Albertina Sisulu's statement that 'leaders try to stop uprisings ... it is the government that wants uprisings' (A. Marx, 1992, p. 35) raises serious questions as to where the logic of national UDF strategy led. The heroic, if sometimes unguided and disorganised, struggles waged by those who answered the call to 'arms' were certainly not carried out to achieve a negotiated settlement for a deracialised capitalism. As one leading community activist put it: 'we believed we were fighting not just for nationalism, but for socialism' (Mayekiso, personal interview, October 1991).

In spite of this, and however much the national structures of the UDF were prepared to accept a negotiated solution, Botha and his securocrats were in no mood for such accommodation. Having already dashed the insurrectionary hopes of the ANC/SACP/UDF, the government crowned its 'victory' by effectively banning the UDF in February 1988. Much of the securocrats' attention was once more focused on the regional and international arenas where they were facing severe military and economic challenges. Ironically, it was in these arenas where Botha and his securocrats were to meet their Waterloo.

The Logic of External Management

Today in many parts of the country, government policy is driving people into resistance to a stage where they are clamoring for action. Local leaders cannot lag behind the people, or they will cease to be leaders and the blind forces of destruction and revenge will take over. But local action must always be principled, in accordance with the established policy and general direction of the national leadership. No desperation, no adventurism, but firm, resolute and revolutionary action. That should be the watchword of the oppressed people and their leaders in the difficult days ahead.

SACP Central Committee (1963)[5]

Even though these directives were given in 1963 they were certainly still relevant for the national liberation movement of the 1980s – the internal upsurge in struggle presented the ANC with a situation which, more than ever, called for 'resolute and revolutionary action' and leadership. The political (and symbolic) hegemony of the externalised liberation movement ensured that the vast majority of those who took up the ANC call to make South Africa ungovernable looked to it for such action and leadership. In this regard, the ANC was greatly aided by vitriolic apartheid propaganda directed at the 'communist terrorists', and the association of virtually any resistance activity with the externalised movement. Although the UDF was the legal organisational structure to which the majority of the internal masses were attached, they looked to the ANC and its armed wing MK to provide them with the means to realise the vision of genuine people's power. How did the ANC respond?

The first and most obvious strategic response of the ANC was to issue the call for ungovernability. Senior strategists saw the potential of this as giving strategic purpose to internal formations and unifying disparate struggles around a vision of people's power. According to NEC member and former head of the ANC Department of Political Education, Raymond Suttner, 'the call to make South Africa ungovernable was the correct strategic insight given the objective conditions at the time' (personal interview, November 1992). Similarly, ANC NEC and SACP Central Committee member Jeremy Cronin has argued:

> The weakness of the internal groupings (their strength lay in the political space which they created), was that they flew in a million different directions. This is why you need a clear political strategy and a unified political formation which surgically directs towards key tasks – this is what the ANC successfully did during the 1980s (for example, the call for ungovernability, the call to a people's war) – it emerged as hegemonic and unifying and gave strategic purpose to the UDF and COSATU-type structures. (personal interview, October 1992)

However much the externalised ANC possessed a 'clear political strategy' and however much it was able, simultaneously, to become 'hegemonic', it is the character of the ANC's strategic response to the mass struggles of the 1980s that matters. There is a substantial difference between identifying key tasks through a clear political strategy and implementing the necessary foundations to support and direct subsequent action. As the April 1985 ANC NEC statement noted, there had to be a unified and disciplined underground organisation capable of providing such support and direction for such strategic calls to have long-term effect. The 'key task', given the prevailing conditions, was to combine armed and mass struggles under the political leadership and strategic organisation of an internal underground. As much as the ANC provided a symbolic and organisational focal point for internal resistance, there could be no real hope of a seizure of power through accumulative people's power as long as that focal point remained predominantly externalised.

During the height of the internal resistance some ANC and SACP strategists, caught up in the insurrectionary mood, pushed the idea that people's organs of power provided the basis for a dual power (competing institutions of governance for example, in townships). It was posited that this dual power was a direct and immediate challenge to the viability of the apartheid state (Mashinini, 1986; Mzala, 1986). As previously noted however, conceptualisations of dual power at the national level assumed the imminent or near-term collapse of the administrative and coercive power of the apartheid state.

Such a perspective was given added impetus by the belief, as expressed by the ANC NEC, that a 'long-lasting work stoppage, backed by our oppressed communities and supported by armed activity, can break the backbone of the apartheid system and bring the regime to its knees' (ANC, 1985, p. 2). Such a call, if effectively implemented, would no doubt have acted as a catalyst for an insurrectionary seizure of power. And yet if there was any hope of bringing 'the regime to its knees' the state's administrative and coercive capacities would, of necessity, have to suffer serious damage. As we have seen, the state's administrative and coercive capacities were not fundamentally undermined by work stoppages, the effects of which fell predominantly on domestic capital. Thus, if such a call were to have the intended effect, the armed component of the liberation movement would have to mount a serious challenge to the armed forces of the apartheid state: a challenge that was never sustained.

Despite the inability of the ANC and its internal allies to broaden and sustain a dual power, ANC strategic and tactical projections provided the background for the activities and expectations of the internal resistance. The extent of the externalised ANC's (and MK's) almost unquestioned moral authority and symbolic power revealed itself in the content and character of internal resistance:

- the youth mimicked armed MK combatants in their one-sided battles with the SADF, 'armed' in most cases with stones, molotov cocktails and wooden AK-47 replicas;
- workers embarked on stoppages, students refused apartheid-controlled schooling and communities attacked representatives of apartheid;
- at every rally, demonstration and funeral the banners and symbols of the ANC and SACP dominated, especially anything associated with Mandela;
- the Freedom Charter became the struggle 'bible', its vaguely worded content allowing myriad interpretations and allegiances.

If all of this gave credence to the ANC's claim to be the 'sole legitimate representative' of the oppressed, then it likewise confirmed that the South African masses expected that the ANC would lead them to the promised seizure of power. While there are those who would no doubt dispute this perspective, it is extremely difficult, given the practical activity of those on the ground, to make the argument that the broad mass was struggling for a negotiated liberation. Such a view seemed to be the preserve of the ANC leadership. As Oliver Tambo stated at the height of the uprising, the ANC's main objective was not 'a military victory but to force Pretoria to the negotiating table' (*Financial Mail*, 17 January 1986).

Whatever differences over the main objective there were between ANC leadership, rank-and-file activists and the ANC's mass base, the way in which the armed struggle continued to be prosecuted virtually ensured there would be no potential insurrectionary seizure of power. The theoretical position adopted by ANC strategists posited that the armed struggle must link up with grassroots mass struggles in order to create the conditions for a people's war. As the SACP had put it, to 'transform "simple" mass uprisings into armed uprisings' (SACP, 1986, p. 3). Despite the substantial increase in the number of MK attacks during the uprising,[6] these attacks continued to be confined overwhelmingly to hit-and-run sabotage operations. The development of autonomous internal armed formations based among the general populace and linked with grassroots structures, was minimal. As one student activist in the Eastern Cape said, there was 'never systematic integration of the mass movement into the armed struggle' (Langa Zita, personal interview, October 1992).

The effectiveness of MK was not helped by organisational feuding and the lack of internal political and military leadership capable of giving direction, discipline, providing supplies and sustaining guerrilla units in the field. SACP and ANC leader Jeremy Cronin gives a good example of the need for internal organisation: he describes how an MK cadre who was employed as a technician in a sensitive government installation in Pretoria had to flee the country after a minor bomb attack on the installation, pointing out that the cadre could have disrupted the entire installation by using his access and technical knowledge to damage sensitive equipment permanently (personal interview, October 1992). Similarly, an internal activist told of how local MK recruits often disregarded elementary security precautions by keeping hand grenades under their beds (Lewis, personal interview, May 1992).

All of this combined to ensure little change in the conduct and results of armed activity despite stated strategic goals. The increased activities of MK did have a significant psychological impact on the black populace, which gave the ANC an invaluable mobilising tool, and these activities certainly contributed to the growing problems of the apartheid state. However, as long as an externalised ANC leadership and strategy and tactics guided MK practice, the scope for developing the conditions for an armed seizure of power was extremely limited.

Whether or not the armed struggle was seen as merely a pressure tactic for eventual negotiation or as a way of realising an armed seizure of power, the externalised ANC was, more than ever, reliant on favourable international conditions to maintain anything resembling a viable military option. In this regard, events in the international arena during the late 1980s increasingly narrowed the scope for the externally based activities of MK, and set the scene for further accommodation.

Although no one could predict Mikhail Gorbachev's rise to power in the USSR in 1985, it signalled a sea change in global power relations and consequently in the ANC's liberation struggle. Within a few months of taking office, Gorbachev had made it clear that it was his intention to force changes in Soviet domestic policy and foreign relations. Stressing the desire for the USSR to free itself from a debilitating Cold War mentality, Gorbachev saw the need to reach agreement with the United States on arms reductions in order to implement his domestic agenda. As part of this plan Gorbachev and President Ronald Reagan met in Iceland in October 1986 where they agreed verbally, among other things, to try to halt military intervention and assistance to favoured allies in the so-called third world. It was an 'agreement' that, under the objective conditions pertaining in their respective countries, greatly favoured the United States.

For the ANC, who had come to rely on the Soviets and East Germans for everything from printing journals to military hardware, this development had three effects: to reduce further its ability to wage an externalised armed struggle; to hasten the implementation of its macro-strategy of negotiations; or to force the ANC to commit itself fully to an internally-based people's war. The last option was a remote possibility, given previously established practice and the logic of the officially chosen national liberation strategy.

Both the ANC and SACP formally welcomed Gorbachev's reforms. For the SACP this was consistent with the leadership's historic, if short-sighted, support of the line from Moscow. Yet, what even the SACP could not foresee was the impact of these changes on southern Africa. Beginning in late 1987 Angolan government troops launched a large-scale offensive against UNITA. As it had done so many times in the past, the apartheid state came to UNITA's aid, and there ensued a brief military standoff. However, the apartheid securocrats, who had become increasingly confident of their military capabilities, decided to push ahead and attempt to make southern Angola a permanent UNITA enclave. In the process they hoped to undermine the MPLA government in Angola (who staunchly supported the ANC), ensure their hold over neighbouring Namibia and consolidate their political supremacy at home.

The military campaign of the SADF/UNITA culminated in what is now known as the battle of Cuito Cuanavale. After several months of intense fighting between the SADF/UNITA and Angolan government troops backed by their Cuban allies around the strategic southern Angolan town of Cuito Cuanavale, the SADF/UNITA forces retreated, having failed to take the town. Indeed, it was the presence of thousands of Cuban troops and their sophisticated air and ground weaponry which eventually turned the tide against the UNITA/SADF forces. Although there continued to be a military standoff along the Angolan–Namibian border, it soon became apparent that the United States and the USSR wanted an end to the fighting.

Immediately following the battle, the United States and the USSR began to hold secret high-level meetings involving their respective southern Africa officials, Chester Crocker and Anatoly Adamishin (Callinicos, 1992, p. 92). These led to a series of further meetings between the Angolans, Cubans and the apartheid state over the possibilities of a signed agreement which would guarantee simultaneous withdrawal of Cuban and South African troops from Angola and Namibia respectively. Under intense pressure from the United States and USSR the sides cut a deal in December 1988 in New York. The outcome had important repercussions for all players in the region.

The New York agreement signalled a serious political setback for Botha and his securocrats. Not only did the Angolan débâcle and subsequent agreement cost them dearly in terms of their Afrikaner political base,[7] but their dominance of the ruling National Party was under attack more than ever from more moderate elements. Although Botha and his securocrats had succeeded in crushing militarily the insurrectionary potential of internal revolt and seriously disrupting the ANC's attempts at conducting external guerrilla warfare (through regional destabilisation), they had never wholly grasped the political and economic realities of apartheid capitalism. In that it continued to believe that it could retain absolute white political dominance while gradually increasing economic opportunities for the black majority, the Botha government was blind to the need for pre-emptive political accommodation which might secure a truncated white political role but which would preserve capitalism. Even though no one could predict with certainty what was going to happen, the moderates who were now knocking on the door of National Party power could not but face the reality that had escaped Botha and his predecessors.

For the ANC the New York agreement meant closing down all of its bases in Angola. Already far from their country, MK cadres would now have to retreat even further to places like Tanzania, Zambia and Uganda. The armed struggle had come full circle. The dislocation of thousands of MK cadres resulted in serious problems for the ANC. As might have been expected there was widespread demoralisation within MK, no doubt linked to reports that the organisation's security department, Mbokodo, was running amok once again (Ellis and Sechaba, 1992, pp. 192–3). Mbokodo had, at one stage, even arrested senior ANC NEC member Pallo Jordan. One young exile termed the state of the externalised ANC as 'a general law of the jungle' (Michael Sachs, personal interview, October 1991).

The New York agreement also made it clear that the USSR was no longer willing to support the armed struggle of the ANC. This should have been a particularly harsh blow for SACP activists since their line had always been that the 'communist' USSR would never abandon the South African revolution. And yet the SACP continued to hold up the USSR as the socialist model. It would take the disintegration of the Soviet empire and 'communist' Eastern Europe finally to force the SACP to come to terms with reality.

These developments represented more than just a severe body blow to the hopes of MK rank and file and movement militants. They signalled the completed logic of the ANC's externally based struggle for national liberation. Having consistently adopted a theory and strategy that resulted in an externally-driven armed struggle whose *raison d'être* was the seizure of power and whose practice mitigated against the development of a politically organised and armed internal underground, the ANC was caught out.

In the midst of these events, senior ANC and SACP leaders had undertaken a plan for building up an internal underground. Named

Operation Vula and begun in the late 1980s, it involved senior ANC and MK leaders clandestinely re-entering South Africa to set up a core political and military cadre. While Operation Vula was part of the long-awaited plan for a sustainable underground capable of directing revolutionary armed struggle, its potential was ostensibly undermined through exposure. Whatever gains Operation Vula had managed to secure (for example, to rejuvenate organisational and military connections between MK and internal activists), it is questionable what commitment the externalised ANC leadership had to utilise those gains. Indeed, the activities already underway on the international and domestic front made it probable that the ANC leadership would choose the route which they had effectively already chosen – negotiation.

The decade of the 1980s, despite all its liberation struggle permutations, had seen the ANC achieve a hegemonic position both inside the country and internationally. However, the strategic character of the ANC's approach to both armed struggle and the internal revolts, plus the ongoing setbacks – both internal and international – which undercut its ability to pose a serious military threat to the apartheid regime, had served to strengthen further an increasingly overt politics of accommodation throughout the 1980s. As a result, it was the terrain of international politics (and capital) that the ANC increasingly turned to during the late 1980s for the realisation of its stated goal of national liberation for the 'transfer of power to the people'.

5

Fourth Pillar, Fifth Column:[1] The Internationalisation of the Struggle

> We have had one goal for seventy-seven years: to get rid of apartheid. Anyone who has accepted that goal has been welcomed into the ANC to join and help us ... Anything which seeks to divide us, whether from the left or the right, seeks to break the unity which the ANC prizes above everything.
>
> Thabo Mbeki[2]

As potential for the insurrectionary seizure of power receded during the 1980s so the prospect of solidifying a politics of accommodation gained momentum. The ANC leadership's prioritisation of the international pillar of its liberation struggle prepared the ground for a very different kind of accession to power from that expected by its cadre and mass constituency.

The character of the ANC's sanctions campaign, framed within an international 'united front' politics, provides the best example of the subsequent strategic convergence that occurred between the liberation movement and international capitalism. By embracing extremely powerful forces which had the clear agenda of creating a deracialised capitalism in South Africa, the ANC's sanctions campaign cemented its historic macro-strategy of accommodation; the liberation movement had reached a strategic impasse and a negotiated path to liberation became a *fait accompli*.

The New Role of Capital

The long-standing crisis of apartheid capitalism, which had provided the structural background for both the actions of the apartheid state and those who struggled against it, had become acute by mid-1985. South Africa's increasing dependence on external finance capital, the internal uprising and Botha's repressive brinkmanship combined to create a situation in which the apartheid state faced a revolt from within – not in the political arena but from leading sections of domestic and international capital. Having benefited handsomely from decades of apartheid policies, but also having recognised for some time the need for substantive deracialisation of the apartheid system, these capitalists now began to look for an indication that the Botha government would commit itself to reform.

At the Natal National Party congress in August 1985 Botha proved that he and his securocrats had not learned the essence of capitalist survival – flexibility. As an expectant domestic and international audience watched, Botha told the world he was 'not prepared to lead White South Africans ... on a road to abdication and suicide', and warned the apartheid state's critics not to 'push us too far' (Schire, 1991, pp. 82–3). However, leading South African capitalists immediately denounced the government's position and called publicly for the scrapping of statutory racial discrimination. They also called for the beginning of negotiations with 'legitimate' black leaders (including domestic capital's favourite son, Gatsha Buthelezi), aimed at power-sharing. More importantly from the apartheid state's perspective however, was the subsequent decision by major international banks to call in government debt. By refusing to roll over South Africa's short-term debt, international financial capital greatly exacerbated an already deep economic crisis. In response, the government temporarily closed the Johannesburg Stock Exchange and imposed a moratorium on the repayment of South Africa's short-term debt, which had soared to over 70 per cent of the total debt of $24 billion (Hirsch, 1989, p. 270). This in turn gave rise to a virtual freeze on international loans to South Africa, led by the American banks. Within months, loans to the apartheid state from these banks fell by nearly half (IRRC, 1989). The South African struggle had gained new passengers.

Although South African capital had consistently issued verbal broadsides against the ANC, deriding the organisation for its 'socialist' outlook, it did not take long before this capital put aside its fears. Within days of the loan freeze a delegation of leading representatives of South African monopoly capital, (including the Premier Group, Barclays Bank, Sanlam and Barlow Rand), led by Anglo American chairman Gavin Relly, travelled to Lusaka to confer with the ANC leadership, including Chris Hani, Thabo Mbeki, Pallo Jordan and Mac Maharaj and led by Oliver Tambo (*Business Day*, 3 September 1985; *Sunday Times*, 15 September 1985). Asked what the talks would be about, Relly stated:

> I think that there is a coherent sense for businessmen to want to find out if there is common ground ... that a free enterprise society is demonstrably better at creating wealth than some type of Marxist socialism. I would have thought it was self-evident ... that nobody wants to play a role in a country where the economy ... was destroyed either by a sort of Marxist approach to wealth creation, or by a ... revolution. (*The Weekly Mail*, 13–19 September 1985)

Commenting on the meeting on the ANC's *Radio Freedom*, Oliver Tambo stated that it had been the 'armed struggle' that had forced Relly and company to come to the ANC. He continued:

> They [domestic capital] ... want to reform the apartheid system in such a way that the end result is a system that secures their business but is minus racial discrimination. And that is what they are looking for; a system that falls short of the stipulations of the Freedom Charter but moves away from a system that thrives on violence and produces counter-violence. Well, we do not think that such a system is different. (Tambo, *Radio Freedom* interview, 15 October 1985)

This assessment was correct; however, Tambo was talking to a converted audience. Even if the ANC leadership genuinely desired the full implementation of the Freedom Charter the logic of its own national democratic conception of struggle, coupled with the economic vagueness of the Charter, found common ground with a deracialised capitalism. As for Relly and his colleagues, they came away with a changed perception of the ANC. Commenting on South African Broadcasting Corporation Radio, Relly said that he had the impression that the ANC was not 'too keen' to be seen as 'marxist', and that he felt they had a good understanding 'of the need for free enterprise' (Relly, *SABC* interview, 14 September 1985). For its part, the ANC leadership seemed unsure about accepting the former enemy's bona fides and issued a statement that decried attempts by 'self-appointed bigwigs, elitists etc. to cobble together settlements of the fate of the country over the heads of the people' (Barrell, *The Weekly Mail*, 27 Sept.– 3 Oct. 1985). Whatever the character of the verbal battle, it was obvious that South African monopoly capital now thought it must, and could, deal with the ANC. For decades the ANC had been making calls for business, and whites in general, to join the struggle against apartheid. Now that the call had been answered in part, the ANC had to deal with two new domestic constituencies: leading sections of South African monopoly capital and white political opinion. Moreover, on the international scene the ANC found itself with two more powerful constituents that it could no longer dismiss through the use of radical rhetoric.

International capital had given the ANC a huge boost by instituting financial sanctions against the apartheid state, and the US government, through the 1986 Schultz (Secretary of State) Report, had concluded that no lasting solution in South Africa was possible without the participation of the ANC (Phillips and Coleman, 1989, p. 13). US Under-Secretary of State Michael Armacost confirmed this new approach by recognising that the ANC was now viewed as the 'legitimate voice of the black community'

(*Sowetan*, 22 December 1986). At the same time that its new constituents were calling for negotiations, the ANC continued to issue strident calls for an insurrectionary seizure of power. The organisation had some fundamental choices to make. But with the potential for overthrowing the apartheid state by force steadily receding, and given the externalised environment within which most of the leadership operated, it was not surprising that the ANC turned more of its efforts and energy to the international front.

The Push for Negotiation

The first indication of how the ANC might respond to calls for negotiation came after the visit by the Commonwealth Eminent Persons Group (EPG) to South Africa early in 1986. The EPG, appointed by the Commonwealth states, included former Nigerian President Olusegun Obasanjo and former Australian Prime Minister Malcolm Fraser. After their visit (where the group was given a decidedly cold reception by the Botha government) the EPG held lengthy discussions with the ANC leadership. During these talks, it was proposed that the potential political space for the legalisation of the ANC and SACP now existed, conditional on the cessation of armed action and the opening of negotiations with Pretoria. According to one informed observer, the ANC was nearing acceptance of these proposals when the apartheid state scuttled any hopes of a negotiated settlement by launching raids on supposed MK bases in the neighbouring countries of Lesotho and Botswana (Lodge, 1987, p. 13).

With the EPG mission in disarray the ANC leadership proceeded to criss-cross the globe between 1986 and 1988 attending a host of international non-governmental and solidarity conferences, meetings with top British, Soviet, Japanese, Australian and US government officials, as well as with prominent Afrikaners. A leading ANC member complained:

> If you went to Lusaka to see a member of the working committee ... you were lucky [to find one] ... the top members of the ANC were permanently in the air [;] ... it had a terrible effect. So in fact this great national leadership of the ANC in Lusaka was really individuals operating in their own departments and in their own way that had a tremendously debilitating effect and it meant that international and solidarity work took priority over everything else. (Turok, personal interview, October 1992)

While the formal content of these meetings most probably consisted of diplomatic exchanges and the sounding out of respective approaches, their real importance lay elsewhere for they represented not only the broad acceptance, by political and economic representatives of capital, that the ANC was the major representative of opposition to the apartheid state but also a coming home of sorts for the ANC leadership. Although the armed struggle would continue to be its main pressure tactic, the ANC leadership was now openly pursuing its wider strategy of seeking a negotiated settlement.

There has been a tendency far too often to explain the ANC's turn to seeking a negotiated settlement as the sole result of difficult objective conditions. Thus it has been claimed that the character of the ANC's national democratic struggle represented a pragmatic realism, since the organisation was operating within the conditions and balance of power considerations as they existed.[3] Such an explanation is crudely structuralist for two reasons: it ignores the possibilities that mass struggle had already created for fundamentally altering the balance of forces; and it creates the impression that the actions and strategies of the ANC leadership had nothing to do with the political choices it made. The fact is that the ANC leadership had made a definitive strategic choice.

With international activity raising questions with regard to the strategic and tactical intentions of the ANC, the leadership needed to provide clarification to its own cadre. Many of the ANC rank and file, especially MK cadres, became suspicious that the leadership unilaterally would enter into negotiations with the apartheid state. One MK cadre, who felt that something was 'drastically wrong', described how the leadership was 'summoned ... and they told us there was no way the ANC would just go into talks. In 1988 the rumours surfaced again and we were again told that there would be no talks' (*The Star*, 28 April 1991). Whatever the leadership told MK cadres in the camps it certainly appeared to be sending a different message to other constituencies. In a statement that appeared in the British newspaper the *Observer* in March 1986, ANC International Affairs head (now Deputy President) Thabo Mbeki stated:

> The call you make to people is the same, saying you are not prepared to negotiate, that you must intensify the offensive. But in the course of that offensive it is clear that one of the most important things is breaking up the power structure ... Out of this you will get a re-alignment of forces. We are not talking of overthrowing the government but of turning so many people against it that it would be forced to do what Ian Smith did.

Mbeki's reference to Ian Smith, former prime minister of Rhodesia, refers to the Lancaster House Settlement in which Smith's neo-apartheid government negotiated the country's independence with the leaders of the two liberation movements, Zimbabwe African National Union – ZANU, and Zimbabwe African People's Union

– ZAPU. It surely could not have escaped Mbeki's attention that the outcome of Zimbabwe's national liberation had led to the very 'result' that the ANC leadership had stated it wanted to avoid – that is, deracialised capitalism. By the mid-1980s it had become apparent that the Zimbabwe government had abandoned any real attempt to transform the social and economic relations of the inherited capitalist system. Indeed, Zimbabwe was well on its way to becoming an important ally of international financial capital through the facilities of the IMF and the World Bank.

In addition, Mbeki's statement came very close to confirming the existence of a double agenda on the part of certain sections of the ANC leadership – at least at the rhetorical level. Mbeki's call cannot be adjudged simply as a strategem designed to reach the ultimate strategic goal of liberation for the 'transfer of power to the people'. An organisation that claims (and is given) a liberation mandate from 'the people' should not be used as a conveyor belt for the strategic (or class) agenda of certain leaders. Similarly, people who answer the calls of those leaders to struggle for their freedom, and who give their lives for the liberation struggle, should not be used as pawns in the chess game of politics, no matter what the rationalisations.

It is important to reiterate here what was behind such apparent contradictions. The main reason that ANC leaders such as Thabo Mbeki pursued these kinds of tactics can be traced to two sources:

- the conscious practice of an externalised, narrowly conceived and racially bound struggle for national liberation which most often led to the presumption of both the will of the people and the potentials of their struggles;
- a neutralised and reactive approach to the prevailing conditions wherein these conditions negate (as part of the dialectic) the possibilities and process of revolutionary struggle.

Mbeki's statement, if fully publicised, would no doubt have been less than heartening to those millions of people in whose name he and the other ANC leaders were leading.

The Mbeki statement was followed by two ANC NEC statements which confirmed that the leadership was willing to enter into negotiations under certain conditions. In its statement of 8 January 1987 the NEC proclaimed: 'we reiterate our commitment to seize any opportunity that may arise to participate in a negotiated resolution of the conflict in our country'. However, it was a special NEC statement on 'The Question of Negotiations' released on 9 October 1987 that set out, for the first time, the ANC's strategic approach. Arguing that the 'racist regime' had raised the issue of negotiations 'to defuse the struggle inside our country' and to 'defeat the continuing campaign for comprehensive and mandatory sanctions', the NEC stated:

> Once more, we would like to reaffirm that the ANC and the masses of our people as a whole are ready and willing to enter into genuine negotiations provided they are aimed at the transformation of our country into a united and non-racial democracy. *This, and only this, should be the objective of any negotiating process.* (original emphasis)

Rejecting the idea of unilaterally suspending the armed struggle, the statement declared that 'any cessation of hostilities would have to be negotiated and entail agreed action by both sides ...'. Noting the 'treacherous and deceitful nature of the apartheid regime', the NEC 'insisted' that 'the apartheid regime would have to demonstrate its seriousness by implementing various measures to create a climate conducive to ... negotiations'. These were:

- the unconditional release of all political prisoners, detainees, all captured freedom fighters and prisoners of war as well as the cessation of all political trials;
- the lifting of the state of emergency and the withdrawal of the army and the police from the townships and their confinement to barracks;
- the repealing of all repressive legislation and all laws empowering the regime to limit freedom of assembly, speech, the press and so on.

In conclusion, the statement affirmed that the ANC was 'opposed to any secret negotiations', because 'we firmly believe that the people themselves must participate in shaping their destiny and would therefore have to be involved in any process of negotiations'.

This NEC statement set the ANC firmly on a negotiations course. By setting out publicly maximum conditions for negotiations the ANC leadership sent a clear signal that it was prepared to engage in compromise. At the same time, in order to strengthen its hand at any future negotiating table, the ANC insisted that the 'struggle' be intensified 'on all fronts' (*Umsebenzi*, Fourth Quarter 1987).

It was thus not surprising that one of the NEC's next statements stressed the 'centrality of the armed struggle', and urged followers to 'transform our offensive into a general people's war' (ANC NEC Statement, 17 August 1988). No doubt such rejoinders were designed in part to reassure the rank and file that they were not being sold out, but they also highlighted one of the historical contradictions attached to the ANC leadership's approach to the national liberation struggle – do as we say, not necessarily as we do.

At the conceptual level, the organisation would now utilise mass struggle and armed action for two specific purposes: to act as pressure levers on the apartheid state in the lead-up to any future negotiations; and to ensure that the mass base was involved in the macro-strategy of a negotiated settlement. It remained to be seen how this would translate into practice.

Finding Common Ground

The most detailed ANC response to any remaining questions concerning the path it had chosen were contained in the organisation's Constitutional Guidelines released in the latter half of 1988 (Lodge and Nasson, 1991, pp. 352–6). Designed to 'convert' the Freedom Charter 'from a vision for the future into a constitutional reality', the Guidelines committed the ANC to a political programme that fell comfortably within the framework of a liberal bourgeois democracy. Calling for a 'unitary state' with distinct executive, judicial and legislative branches, and the guarantee of individual human rights through a Bill of Rights, the ANC envisaged a 'democratic and non-racial' South Africa (p. 353). On the economic front the Guidelines were once again consistent with a liberal bourgeois outlook. It was stated that 'the economy will be a mixed one', and that there would be constitutional protection of 'property for personal use and consumption'. As for the role of the state, it would ensure that the 'entire economy serves the interest and well being of the entire population' (p. 355).

In broad terms the Guidelines represented ideological continuity with the Freedom Charter. However, the ANC had now provided a more specifically defined vision of political pluralism and civil liberties in a post-apartheid South Africa, while the economic clauses represented a change from the Freedom Charter formulations. Nationalisation had now been replaced with an even more vague notion of the role of the state having 'the right to determine the general context in which economic life takes place' and in which the 'private sector of the economy shall be obliged to co-operate with the state ... in promoting social well-being' (p. 355).

The Guidelines confirmed the ANC's acceptance of a negotiated path to national liberation (no liberation movement which foresees itself forcibly overthrowing the enemy has ever pre-emptively revealed constitutional guidelines). More importantly though, the Guidelines showed that the practical strategies adopted by the ANC (formally enshrined at Morogoro) were, in the final analysis, fundamentally linked to an accommodative, negotiated national liberation. After failing to come anywhere close to an armed seizure of power, the ANC was now reverting to its historical path of accommodative politics, trusting that the continued activity of its mass base would ensure a generally progressive outcome.

It should be noted that the core message emanating from the youth and workers inside the country at the time was for a socialist revolution. If the ANC leadership had polled its own constituency and allowed the active involvement of this mass base in drawing up the Guidelines, it would surely have produced a very different document. The general response to this gap between the visions of the broad masses and the leadership has often been to defend the Guidelines as a tactical move designed to appeal to the broadest spectrum of opinion and ensure a smooth transition to national democracy (the first stage of liberation). However, it must be remembered that ANC (and SACP two-stage) theory and practice in essence demanded a united-front strategy. The Constitutional Guidelines, far from being a short-term tactical manoeuvre, represented the logical extension of the ANC's long-term strategy.

What is noteworthy about both the NEC statement on negotiations and the Constitutional Guidelines is the absence of any mention of the role and influence (both present and future) of international and domestic monopoly capital and their political representatives. It was as though the ANC leadership viewed the liberation struggle as one of pitting the global forces of moral good against evil apartheid. In the meantime, however, powerful international capital did not simply sit on the sidelines waiting for the ANC and the apartheid state to come to terms. International capital was making moves to court the ANC leadership away from any adherence it might still have to socialist struggle. In addition, even before the ANC had publicly released their conditions for negotiations, Gavin Relly let it be known that domestic monopoly capital had its own agenda for a 'new' South Africa. While chiding the ANC for its continued adherence to sanctions, Relly sounded as though he was pre-empting the NEC's statement by arguing that:

> Among ourselves [monopoly capital] we have reached agreement that statutory apartheid must go, that the political process be opened up by the release of prisoners of conscience, that political parties, currently banned, be allowed to operate within the rule of law and that real attempts be made for constructive negotiation between all parties in South Africa. (Relly, 1986)

Relly's attack on the ANC is understandable but somewhat misplaced. The financial sanctions instituted by international financial capital were creating serious credit problems for domestic business and Relly's call for a political settlement was no doubt designed to create a stability which would result in the lifting of those financial sanctions. While the ANC certainly had a degree of international moral influence, the dependent factor as far as the lifting of financial sanctions was concerned lay with getting the ANC to the negotiating table rather than with the degree of moral suasion which the organisation could continue to muster.

Earlier in the year another Anglo American executive, Zach de Beer, had provided the rationale for monopoly capital's agenda. He had told the Royal Commonwealth Society:

> We all understand how years of apartheid have caused many blacks to reject the economic as well as the political system. But we dare not allow the baby of free enterprise to be thrown out with the bathwater of apartheid. (*Financial Times*, UK, 10 June 1986)

On the international front the US government, which was now acting as the major international political powerbroker in Southern Africa, had grasped the necessity of creating a climate conducive to the ANC accepting a negotiated settlement. Part of this effort included the upgrading of its so-called development assistance to South African blacks. This development aid consisted of financial assistance to a 'Human Rights Fund', a 'Labor Union Training' project run by the African-American Labor Institute of the Union Federation AFL-CIO (previously denounced by the SACP as a front for the CIA), the 'Special Self-Help Fund' for 'community development'; higher education programmes for students to study in the US and funds for 'strengthening democratic institutions' run by the National Endowment for Democracy (another institution known for its close links to the CIA).[4]

It does not take a close analysis to conclude that this development aid was an integral part of the US government's attempts to propagandise the benefits of 'free enterprise' and bring South Africa into the Western capitalist camp. Indeed, the US government did not try to hide its desire to find ways of influencing the ANC. In a report to Congress, entitled 'Communist Influence in South Africa', the State Department argued that pressure for a negotiated solution would weaken the cohesion of the ANC and implied that this might result in a moderate/radical split within the organisation (State Department Report, 1987, pp. 90–9). Such a split was no doubt seen by the US government and international capital as desirable in order to pull the 'moderates' further towards being part of an acceptable solution (that is, a deracialised capitalism).

The implications of these agendas were not completely unrecognised within the ANC leadership. In mid-1986 Joe Slovo warned of a potential dilemma for the organisation: 'premature speculation about possible compromises in order to tempt broader forces such as the liberal bourgeoisie on to our side may serve to blunt the edge of the people's revolutionary militancy' (Lodge and

Nasson, 1991, p. 188). Mac Maharaj also recognised the implicit economic rationale of such agendas:

> monopoly capital has demonstrated some concern about the overall implications of the drift towards escalating destabilisation. Its concern is similar to that of the major imperialist powers who are preoccupied about the absence of a stable political solution to guarantee the long term future of capitalism in both South Africa and Southern Africa. (Maharaj, 1988, p.16)

Despite these warnings, the ANC leadership did not pay very close attention to its own analyses – though such analyses could be little more than cautionary rejoinders in the face of the strategic choice the liberation movement had already made to seek an accommodative solution to the liberation struggle. What the West knew, and what the ANC leadership seemingly refused to confirm, was that a negotiated settlement under the prevailing conditions would greatly enhance the possibility of instituting a deracialised capitalism in South Africa. While the US State Department worried about the Trojan horse SACP springing the 'second stage' on unsuspecting 'moderates', they no doubt took solace in the fact that a successful transition to deracialised capitalism would substantially undermine any possible foundation for a socialist South Africa.

It is important to note at this point that during the mid- to late 1980s there was a tendency among academic observers of South Africa and the ANC to misinterpret the logic of liberation theory and practical strategy – a tendency that led to an underplaying of the influence of Western governments and monopoly capital. The result was that the ANC's strategic path was seen as being bound to a national liberation which would deliver radical political and economic transformation (Fatton, 1984, pp. 57–82). Such an approach, like many other analyses of national liberation movements over the last four decades, allows hopes to cloud clear analytical vision. The unfortunate result has been deep-seated disillusionment, the results of which continue to impair contemporary radical scholarship and mass struggle.

The fact is that the ANC had taken the negotiations plunge and more than ever relied on international pressure to force the apartheid state to do the same. At the helm of such international pressure was the sanctions movement, and it was this weapon that had increasingly become the focal point of the ANC's international pillar of struggle.

Prioritising Sanctions

At the heart of any discussion of the use of sanctions as a political and economic weapon is the question of imperialism. Whether taken in its specific or more generalised form, imperialism relates to the global role and character of monopoly capital and, correspondingly, to the activities of capitalist states. The practical effect of imperialism, itself a logical outcome of capitalist development, manifests itself in several ways:

- the servicing of the accumulative needs of an increasingly monopolised capital, particularly financial capital;
- the use of capitalist state power to create optimum conditions for such accumulation on a global scale;
- the use of political and economic intervention in order to mediate the crises that arise in capitalist states from monopoly capital's own form of accumulation (for example, through the IMF and World Bank).

The relevance of imperialism to the question of sanctions is all the more important in the context of South Africa's highly inter-nationalised political economy. In such a context a sanctions campaign has the potential to deepen the existing dependence of the (apartheid) state on international capital inputs. Specifically, financial sanctions emanating from highly centralised international financial capital would have the most direct effect on an apartheid South Africa, heavily (and consciously) dependent as it was, and still is, on access to international sources of financial capital. The corresponding impact of trade and other types of sanctions, while having the potential to cause economic disruptions, would be minimal in contrast, being dependent for any potential success on the concerted adherence of numerous governments and international institutions. As will become clear, the sanctions campaign of the ANC, in mirroring the organisation's united front anti-apartheid approach, allowed the international struggle to be heavily influenced by the very international forces whose interests were opposed to any radical economic transformation in South Africa.

Beginning in the 1950s, the ANC had appealed to the international community to implement boycotts of South African products in order to register its moral opposition to apartheid. This was soon expanded to calls for the UN General Assembly to implement comprehensive and mandatory trade and arms boycotts on the apartheid state. However, it was not until 1977 that the UN Security Council imposed a mandatory arms boycott, and only in 1985 that the Council urged the General Assembly to impose comprehensive trade sanctions (Schmidt, 1987). Besides its efforts at the UN the ANC relied on more friendly nations, in particular the Scandinavian countries, and solidarity organisations such as the British Anti-Apartheid Movement (AAM) in the West to carry the sanctions struggle forward. Most of these efforts, though, were concentrated on attempts to encourage governments to implement arms, trade, political, cultural and sporting boycotts and to force multinational corporations to disinvest – all with varying degrees of (but generally limited) success.

Indeed, the apartheid state was quite successful in getting around the trade and arms boycotts, striking deals with 'offenders' such as the US, Israel, Britain and Japan (for example, providing the US with cheap raw uranium in return for advanced nuclear components) (Mokoena, 1993). Likewise, many corporations succeeded in circumventing the full effects of disinvestment by setting up subsidiaries and using third parties as investment conduits (Africa Research Centre, 1989, pp. 99–104). While many governments voluntarily acceded to the ANC's international sanctions campaign, their reasons for doing so were just as often for self-interest. For example, the Australian government, which vigorously backed the sanctions call, had every reason to want South African coal off the global market to benefit its own large-scale coal production. Although the ANC's sanctions campaign received widespread support its effect had yet, in the words of Oliver Tambo, 'to deny the regime the means through which it can sustain and perpetuate itself' (ANC, 1986). It took the 'voluntary' implementation of financial sanctions by international finance capital in mid-1985 to register a substantive economic impact on apartheid capitalism. Until that time the ANC had had little success in getting financial sanctions imposed on the apartheid state. After the refusal of international finance capital to roll over the government's short-term debt – a decision based on an assessment of the parlous state of the apartheid political economy – the ANC began to pay more attention to the potential of specific financial sanctions. With other types of sanctions having limited economic effect, the ANC and its international anti-apartheid allies began a far more concerted financial sanctions campaign. From 1986 to 1989 there were several failed attempts to halt successive debt rescheduling deals between the state and creditor institutions (ELTSA, 1989, pp. 4–6). Two other demands made by the ANC-led financial sanctions campaign – no new loans and no trade finance – met with more success, although they did not have as strong an effect as the total halt on debt rescheduling.

What was clear, though, was that international finance capital, even with pressure from an array of Western anti-apartheid forces, would ultimately base its decisions on what it considered to be in its own self-interest. While international financial institutions clearly understood the political mileage they could obtain from being seen as anti-apartheid, their main concerns were the longer-term security of their assets and continued access to the South African market. The bankers and financiers knew that because of its structural dependence on external finance the apartheid state would sooner or later have to make the necessary political reforms in order to avert economic collapse. As a financial sanctions report commissioned by the Australian government and endorsed by the ANC and its anti-apartheid allies clearly enunciated:

> It is one of the ironies of the peace process in southern Africa that it owes its existence, at least in part, to the actions of western bankers ... What the financial sanction has done is to reinforce tendencies that were already present in apartheid itself [;] ... the financial sanction works with and not against tendencies inherent in the economy of international finance. South Africa is being excluded from the world stock of savings not because bankers and financiers are ideologically united in their detestation of apartheid ... but because most of them now see South Africa as a bad risk. [T]he financial sanction is almost ideal, because ... it is by and large a sanction that market forces work to encourage. (Ovenden and Cole, 1989, pp. 188–90)

Misplaced Reliance

The practical result of the financial sanctions campaign was a strategic convergence (albeit not a planned one) between the ANC-led international anti-apartheid forces and Western governments, banks and international financial institutions.[5] By the late 1980s all these parties desired the end of apartheid (albeit for different reasons) and all were agreed that a negotiated settlement was by far the best way to achieve this. International financiers and bankers began to set preconditions for South Africa's renewed access to global financial markets: the unbanning of the main black political organisations; the release of political prisoners; the lifting of the state of emergency; a commitment to end all violence; and the beginning of 'meaningful' negotiations (Trewhela, 1990, p. 204). These international actors were also keenly aware that there were sections of the ANC leadership with whom they might find common ideological ground. As a high-ranking SACP official admitted, the activities of these international forces were no doubt partly designed to 'explore the possibilities of a comprador bourgeoisie' (Cronin, personal interview, October 1992).

One of the major reasons why such a convergence developed was the way in which the ANC approached the sanctions question. While correctly identifying the (financial) Achilles' heel of the apartheid state and the historical rationale for foreign investment in South Africa, the implementation of the ANC's sanctions campaign lacked politically strategic foresight and was fundamentally biased towards independent action by state and capital. As a result the

ANC's united front sanctions strategy took control of the sanctions movement (and by consequence the strategy of negotiations) away from both the liberation movement and the broad mass of workers and unemployed who were most affected by it. A grassroots-led campaign would no doubt have been much more empowering to those suffering from the policies of international finance capital, and the ANC would have been in a much stronger position to tackle international financial capital in the long term had it initially adopted such a focus.

The character of the financial sanctions campaign allowed international financial capital to serve its own interests while at the same time championing reform. The degree to which it was able to play both sides of the coin was demonstrated in mid-1989 when financial institutions and banks announced a rescheduling of South Africa's debt before the ANC and its international allies were able to mount an effective campaign against such a move (something they had been planning for a while). Through this action international finance capital went a long way to preserving South Africa's future access to global financial markets and its own access to a lucrative source of accumulation (for example, debt repayments) and to trumping the ANC in the reform pressure stakes.

With the impetus for a sanctions strategy resting squarely on the shoulders of foreign states and international financial capital, the politics of the sanctions movement became increasingly removed from the ANC's base constituency. As a result the sanctions strategy 'created its own parameters' which necessitated the jettisoning of elements of internal mass struggle and organisation (Alexander, personal interview, June 1992). In particular, the leading role of the working class, which the ANC and SACP had continuously reaffirmed in their theoretical formulations and strategic statements, became virtually non-existent.[6]

Even though there was a general uncritical acceptance of the ANC sanctions strategy among the Alliance's leadership, some workers were not convinced. At the 1987 COSATU congress a sanctions resolution was passed by delegates which emphatically declared that the 'organised working class in South Africa have not had control of sanctions campaigns' (Africa Research Centre, 1989, p. 98). Similarly, an article in the *S.A. Metalworker* argued:

> The [sanctions] campaign overseas has been run as if the working class in South Africa had no independent demands. Most importantly the campaign is being run as if workers themselves had no power to control the foreign companies ... The campaign ignores the fact that workers in trade unions have fought long and bitter struggles to have some say in the way in which their lives are organized ... Surely the issue for workers

is not the amount invested or where it comes from, but how workers can begin to control these investments so as to make a real contribution to the struggle to create a South Africa which is free from capitalist oppression and exploitation. (Africa Research Centre, 1989, pp. 37–8)

While the ANC continued to preach the gospel of internal mass struggle and organisation, people's power and the leading role of the working class, its practice did not match its rhetoric. The sanctions-*cum*-negotiations strategy had limited the influence and role of the broad mass and independent working class – the sole constituencies capable of resisting those forces intent on delivering a truncated national liberation. Unfortunately however, the die was cast, and the ANC leadership was not going to let anything or anybody stand in its way.

Towards February 1990

While the externalised ANC leadership was trying to find an acceptable way to the negotiating table, the individual incarnation of the organisation and its struggle, Nelson Mandela, was busy doing the same from inside his prison cell. Following the lead of his organisation, Mandela had first suggested the route of negotiations to his captors in 1986. Acting as a conduit between the apartheid state and the external leadership, Mandela began to assume the mantle of leadership of the ANC once more – a development that was hastened when Oliver Tambo suffered a debilitating stroke in August 1989.

Before his meeting with Botha in mid-1989, Mandela submitted a lengthy letter to the state which revealed for the first time that the ANC was willing to compromise on its basic guiding principle of liberation struggle – majority rule. Accusing the apartheid state of not being serious about negotiations due to its demand that the ANC renounce violence, Mandela sent a clear message of accommodation: 'The truth is that the government is not yet ready for negotiation and for *the sharing of political power* with blacks' (*Guardian*, UK, 26 January 1990; emphasis added)

At virtually the same time as the Mandela letter was being read by the Botha government the SACP was holding its seventh congress in Havana, Cuba. While Mandela was chiding the apartheid state for not entering into negotiations with the ANC and offering a vision of power-sharing, the SACP had this to say:

all-round mass action, merging with organised armed activity, led by a well-organised underground and international pressures, are the keys to the build-up for the seizure of power. Seizure of power will be a product of escalating and progressively merging mass political and military struggle with the likelihood of culminating in an insurrection.

On possible negotiations the SACP stated:

> We should be on our guard against the clear objective of our ruling class and their imperialist allies who see negotiation as a way of preempting a revolutionary transformation. The imperialists seek their own kind of transformation which goes beyond the reform limits of the present regime but which will, at the same time, frustrate the basic objectives of the struggling masses. *And they hope to achieve this by pushing the liberation movement into negotiations before it is strong enough to back its basic demands with sufficient power on the ground.* (*Umsebenzi*, Second Quarter 1989, pp. 11–12; original emphasis)

This 'seizure of power' language was out of step with the reality on the ground, but it did not mean that rank-and-file cadres were merely playing with words. Many still genuinely held to the belief that an armed overthrow of the apartheid state was the only way to achieve liberation. That they continued to do so is testimony to their commitment to radical transformation and to the leadership's unwillingness to face up to strategic realities. The apparent duality within the externalised liberation movement revealed once again that while the immediate outcome of the organisation's liberation struggle was not without its internal critics the strategic path followed possessed a specific logic bound to a politics of accommodation, objective conditions notwithstanding.

Hard on the heels of Mandela's overtures (which were not immediately answered by an ailing and politically weakened Botha), the ANC, along with its internal allies, drafted what came to be known as the Harare Declaration.[7] The drafting of this Declaration came soon after an extensive conference held in Lusaka (29 June–2 July) between top ANC and SACP leaders and a large delegation from the Five Freedoms Forum (a loose-knit South African non-governmental organisation dominated by white liberals). While there was nothing sinister about the meeting and talking with wide sectors of South African society, the conference went far beyond the level of informal discussion. Indeed, the proceedings of the conference and the subsequent Declaration clearly reveal substantive links between the input of the Five Freedoms Forum delegation to central constitutional and policy issues and the text of the Harare Declaration (Louw, 1989).

Combining the 1987 NEC statement on negotiations with the 1988 Constitutional Guidelines, the Harare Declaration made explicit the ANC's desire for a negotiated settlement. Arguing that a 'political settlement' leading to a 'non-racial democracy' had always been the 'preference of the majority of the people of South Africa', the document declared:

> We believe that a conjuncture of circumstances exists which, if there is demonstrable readiness on the part of the Pretoria regime to engage in negotiations genuinely and seriously, could create the possibility to end apartheid through negotiations. (Institute for Black Research, 1993, p. 261)

The conditions under which such negotiations could take place remained the same as those previously stated by the NEC, and it was reiterated that any suspension of the armed struggle would have to come through a negotiated 'mutually binding cease-fire' (Institute for Black Research, 1993, p. 264). The document concluded by laying out the ANC's vision for the formation of an interim government to draw up a new constitution and supervise elections.

The Harare Declaration was the culmination of the organisation's own choice of political strategy for national liberation and further reflected the multitude of pressures and influence of international forces. Ever since the insurrectionary potential of the internal uprising had been crushed effectively and the apartheid state had wreaked havoc through its policy of regional destabilisation, a troubled ANC leadership had turned increasingly to its international pillar of struggle. The pressures for a negotiated settlement had correspondingly increased from all quarters: from the battered Frontline states, from Western governments, from international and domestic capital, from a rapidly disintegrating USSR, and from liberal 'supporters'. With any hopes for a seizure of power a remote possibility along with the organisation's ability to build a viable internal underground linked to armed struggle, the ANC's negotiation strategy was a *fait accompli*.

ANC leaders, in an effort to present the Harare Declaration as a popular expression of the desires of the oppressed, began to make a virtue out of what was really a specific strategic choice. Negotiations were now presented as a 'new terrain of struggle' for power, whose character and direction would be 'determined by the masses' (Carolus, 1989). It was stressed that negotiations should be seen not as replacing armed and mass struggle, but rather as complementing them. Although the extent to which this would be the case remained to be seen, the ANC had passed the point of no return. Given the general state of the external organisation and the combined international and regional pressures it now faced, a negotiated settlement was really the only route it could take. As if to confirm this, on 18 January 1990 ANC Secretary-General Alfred Nzo mistakenly read to a group of journalists an internal document which admitted that the ANC did not have 'the capacity within our country to intensify the armed struggle in any meaningful way' (*Independent*, UK, 19 January 1990).

In coming to this strategic impasse the ANC had not merely been a helpless hostage to the crushing weight of objective conditions. As has been argued, the historic wider strategy of the ANC leadership had been one of accommodation (Thabo Mbeki preferred to call it one of negotiation). The leadership was now tacitly admitting that the varying tactics used (for example, armed struggle) were only part of an overall strategy of negotiation which was, of course, what the people had wanted all along. This book has made the case for viewing the 'objective reality' of a negotiated liberation as the result of conscious strategic choices made by the ANC leadership (that is, the ways in which they conceived of, and led, the liberation struggle). What might have been preferable to negotiation (for example, an insurrectionary triumph of people's power) was possible only to the extent that the character and conduct of the liberation struggle, as practised by the ANC, was determined by those in whose name it was being waged.

While the externalised ANC leadership was doing all it could to facilitate negotiation, the apartheid state was moving in a similar direction. The National Party had jettisoned P.W. Botha (who had recently suffered a stroke) in late 1989 and replaced him with the more reform-minded F.W. de Klerk. De Klerk immediately let it be known that things would be different under his leadership by consciously allowing greater freedom of activity. With the Mass Democratic Movement (MDM – the new name for the reconstituted UDF) structures inside the country having embarked on a new defiance campaign to put pressure on the apartheid state, de Klerk responded by backing off from his predecessor's overt repression and confrontation by allowing more freedom of association and speech. Emboldened by the political space thus created, the MDM held a national Conference for a Democratic Future in December 1989 at which the Harare Declaration was formally adopted. The ANC's internal allies had formally jumped on board the negotiation train.

Acutely aware of the need to stem the continuing economic and political crisis of apartheid capitalism, and faced with mounting internal and international pressures to move towards serious negotiation, de Klerk made his first move by releasing seven prominent ANC leaders in October 1989. This was followed by an international diplomatic offensive designed to lessen South Africa's isolation and give the impression that the new government was committed to change.

It was becoming increasingly clear that de Klerk and his advisers had grasped the need to make a decisive break with past political practice. If there was going to be any chance of dealing with the crisis of apartheid capitalism, de Klerk knew that he would have to pursue a political settlement with the ANC. For its part, the ANC (alongside its internal allies), despite its internal weaknesses and its inability to present a serious armed threat to the apartheid state, had emerged from the 1980s as politically hegemonic. As the main opponents of the apartheid state, the ANC, SACP and the union movement were central to any negotiated settlement.

Although no one could have known the speed with which de Klerk would move, one thing was clear: by releasing Mandela and engaging an ANC leadership committed to a peaceful negotiated settlement, de Klerk would give the white ruling class the best chance to maintain substantial political and economic control over the ensuing process.

6

Returning Home: The Strategy and Practice of Accommodation (1990–93)

> In general, social reforms can never be brought about by the weakness of the strong; they must and will be called to life by the strength of the weak.
>
> Karl Marx[1]

F.W. de Klerk's address to Parliament on 2 February 1990, in which he announced the unbanning of the ANC and SACP and invited them to enter negotiations on South Africa's future, expressed both the apartheid state's and capital's desire to seize the strategic initiative of a process which would lead to a deracialised capitalism. When the ANC leadership responded positively, it placed itself on a political terrain for which it was unprepared. Without any effective control or influence over the state's coercive apparatus, the leadership painted itself into a narrow negotiation-centric corner.

Notwithstanding its various tactical manoeuvres, the ANC could resort to the threat and occasional use of mass struggle only in order to push the negotiations along: the parameters of the struggle were set. The liberation movement was being brought 'home' – laying the groundwork for the institutionalisation of the ANC's historic strategy of incorporation and accommodation (now framed within the search for consensus). The role of the people was secondary.

Calling the ANC's Bluff

When the all-white Parliament opened on 2 February 1990 crowds of demonstrators gathered outside – as they had always done – carrying the banners of opposition organisations and chanting slogans about the illegitimacy of yet another apartheid government. In spite of the belief that de Klerk was being forced to retreat from the bad old days of the 1980s, almost everyone anticipated another presidential speech which would rationalise the political status quo. While the ANC and its internal allies had for some time vigorously been pushing for negotiations to open, their experience of struggle seemed to rule out any strategically astute action by the apartheid state.

What the demonstrators outside Parliament and the externalised ANC had not fully considered was de Klerk's political wile and the fact that he was in a much stronger position than many realised. The ANC (and its followers) had been lulled by its own sense of moral authority. While rightfully claiming that the bitter and heroic struggles waged had made it impossible for the apartheid state to rule in the old way, the reality was that the ANC itself had reached a strategic impasse, and de Klerk knew it. The ANC might have been at the apex of its international and domestic moral authority, but in the harsh world of realpolitik, it was in a weak position, having put most of its cards on the table. F.W. de Klerk, on the other hand still had a strong hand and his first play was to call the ANC's bluff.

De Klerk's parliamentary speech was a master stroke. Citing the changes in the USSR and Eastern Europe – as well as the reduced threat of the liberation movements to 'internal security' and their 'new approach' – de Klerk declared that 'the season of violence is over' and the time had come for 'reconstruction and reconciliation'. From now on, the ANC, SACP, PAC and a host of other allied organisations were free to operate inside the country and Nelson Mandela would now be released. De Klerk then went on to outline the government's agenda for a post-apartheid South Africa, stressing the need to protect minority rights, release the dynamism of market forces, encourage foreign investment and create a peaceful and stable environment for economic and political development. Describing the aims of the government as 'acceptable to all reasonable South Africans', de Klerk carefully laid out his agenda:

> Among other things, those aims include a new, democratic constitution; universal franchise; no domination; equality before an independent judiciary; the protection of minority as well as individual rights; freedom of religion; a sound economy based on proven economic principles and private enterprise; dynamic programmes directed at better education, health services, housing and social conditions for all. (de Klerk, 1990)

De Klerk had put himself (and the apartheid state) in the best possible position to control the negotiated transition to a post-apartheid dispensation. With effective control of the transition, the interests and long-term domination of the white capitalist ruling class would best be assured. Likewise, the continued existence of a still powerful coercive security apparatus in the hands of the apartheid state would act as the ultimate guarantor of an outcome favourable to that class.

It was clear that de Klerk, unlike his predecessors, understood the need to link the interests of the two main components of the ruling class (that is, the white, bureaucratic-apartheid and private capitalist components). He was therefore willing to ditch the

National Party's historic patronage of the Afrikaner working class and to concentrate on appealing to capitalist and petit-bourgeois class interests across racial lines. The practical application of this perspective was to develop over the next three years, gradually becoming a sophisticated programme of coercion, cooption and compromise (more or less in that order).

For the ANC, 2 February, although unexpected, was a godsend. De Klerk however, could not have anticipated the full effect that the events in Eastern Europe and the USSR had had on the ANC and SACP. Besides the obvious loss of military and financial assistance, the collapse of a Stalinist-inspired 'socialism' was a severe blow to those in the liberation movement who had looked to the USSR as the model for transforming South Africa. Whole generations of ANC and SACP cadres had been reared on a steady diet of Stalinist, commandist 'socialism', and when it all disintegrated they were left in an ideological vacuum. The accompanying disillusionment, combined with the new conditions of negotiation, made the movement more susceptible than ever to a strategic and ideological accordance.

The Fetishisation of Talks

Immediately after the release of Mandela on 11 February the ANC and its allies moved to take de Klerk up on his offer. A headquarters was set up in Johannesburg and an 'Interim Leadership Group', consisting of Mandela (appointed Deputy-President of the ANC) and other internal leaders (mainly UDF)[2] was constituted. Although the ANC stressed that all forms of struggle would remain in place, the initial actions of the organisation seemed to confirm that talks would be given priority. The first talks took the form of a series of personal meetings between de Klerk and Mandela – a pattern that was to continue throughout the negotiation process. At the same time, the external leadership was consumed with the task of preparing for its own return for impending negotiations with the government.

While the ANC was preoccupied with talks and internal organisational matters, its supporters were subjected to a torrent of violence from several quarters:

- in the apartheid-created 'homeland' of Bophutatswana ANC supporters were detained and harassed;
- in Gatsha Buthelezi's Kwa-Zulu 'homeland' violent clashes between supporters of the Inkhata movement and the ANC/SACP/UDF (raging since 1986) increased in their intensity and brutality;

- in the townships around Johannesburg violent attacks on actual or potential ANC supporters took place, often perpetrated by Inkhata-aligned hostel dwellers abetted by the state security forces.

Indeed, the 'new' situation provided maximum opportunities for the apartheid state and its proxy forces to conduct a two-tier strategy – the use of violence and negotiation – which would weaken the ANC-led Alliance on the ground and it was hoped at the negotiations table as well.

ANC members and supporters began to appeal to the organisation and its leadership for support against what they clearly saw as a conscious attempt by the apartheid state to weaken and intimidate the organisation's grassroots support base. However, seemingly undeterred by the scale and character of the violence, the ANC leadership continued with its plans for bilateral discussions with the government, as Mandela assured the faithful that de Klerk was a man of integrity who could be trusted.

The violence and the ANC leadership's response were an important barometer for several reasons:

- it highlighted the historical failure of the ANC's struggle to weaken substantively the apartheid security forces and thus have the capacity to demand unconditionally, from the very beginning of the negotiation process, the force's effective restructuring and political neutralisation. MK's ability to check abuses by the apartheid security forces was minimal and, in any case, the ANC's strategic approach had greatly undermined the capacity for an armed support base able to defend the broad mass. This resulted in the ANC's mass base being vulnerable to violent repression and coercive manipulation and having to depend on these same enemy forces to 'control' the violence;
- it revealed that the ANC leadership felt it necessary to rely on talks as the strategic locus for solving problems and achieving power;
- it showed the gap between mass expectations created by the character of the ANC's liberation struggle and the organisation's ability and willingness to meet those expectations. Indeed, one of the main outcomes of the ANC's armed propaganda campaign and the accompanying symbolic appeal of MK heroism was the emergence of a mythology of the armed struggle. There was a widespread expectation that MK would be able not only to protect the people, but also to act as insurance for the fundamental transformation of South Africa.

Without an effective response from the ANC the violence once again served to encourage the youth to take matters into their own hands and, in the process, to foment opposition to the nascent negotiation process. Even though this early violence and the subsequent action taken by the ANC leadership have not received much analysis, at the time it was clear that the only way in which certain of the ANC and allied MDM leadership could hope to control their own constituencies, marginalise troublesome radicals and realise their vision of a national democracy was by pushing ahead with a negotiated settlement.

It is instructive to revisit the question of class in respect to most of the ANC leadership and what this meant in terms of the negotiated transition strategies being pursued. Whether or not the majority of the leadership were located within the petty bourgeoisie in 1990, the politics practised by those at the top certainly reflected a petit-bourgeois mentality. As has been made clear in this book, this meant a politics in which access to institutionalised political and economic power was pursued regardless of the tactics utilised. As former ANC President Dr Xuma had made clear, the political agenda of petit-bourgeois leadership was not to struggle in order to transform capitalism fundamentally, but rather, as the political representatives of popular mass formations, to 'fight and struggle to get our full share and benefit from the system' (Fine and Davis, 1990, p. 52).

While the violence continued unabated, the ANC and apartheid state delegations met for the first time in Cape Town on 4 May 1990. Billed as 'talks about talks', the meeting produced the Groote Schuur Minute, which somewhat nebulously addressed the demands raised by the Harare Declaration. Sounding very similar to what the ANC had years earlier denounced as the cooptive agenda of capital, the Minute stated that 'the government and the ANC agree on a common commitment towards the resolution of the existing climate of violence and intimidation from whatever quarter', and to create a stable and 'peaceful process of negotiations'. The rest of the document briefly dealt with: the issue of political prisoners; immunity for opposition leaders and activists; the lifting of the state of emergency; and the establishment of a working group to make further recommendations. It was agreed that the two sides would meet again soon and 'the objectives contained in this minute' would be 'achieved as early as possible' (ANC, 1990b, pp. 52–3).

As the first formal meeting between the government and the ANC the Groote Schuur talks were notable for the context in which they took place and the limited content of the subsequent Minute. Although the Harare Declaration had set out demands for a 'climate conducive to negotiations', it had been clear that, given the opportunity, the ANC leadership was more than willing to abandon its decades-long external base and enter into institutionalised negotiation. When the delegations met in Cape Town, the ANC, despite threats to the contrary, had little alternative to a negotiated strategy. The Groote Schuur Minute revealed the weakness of the ANC which was now having to play on a completely different field with an entirely different set of rules from what it had experienced for the previous 30 years. In effect, the ANC's demands were more like pleas to the apartheid state to play fairly, while de Klerk had the ability to set the broad rules of the game. To the ANC supporter on the ground the Groote Schuur Minute gave little indication that the ANC was dealing with the apartheid state from a position of strength and would deliver a liberation which reflected the demands of the people.

In between the Groote Schuur talks and the next scheduled meeting with the government in Pretoria, set for 6 August, Mandela set off on the first of many overseas trips. As the international symbol of the South African liberation struggle, Mandela was feted as a hero wherever he went and was able to secure considerable pledges of financial assistance from foreign governments and international corporations. In the United States Mandela wooed business leaders with his pledge to respect free enterprise, and reacted positively to a plan put forward by the President of the Rockefeller Foundation, Peter Goldmark, for the establishment of a development bank for South Africa, funded by foreign investment (*Wall Street Journal*, 25 June 1990). What was particularly interesting about Mandela's receptiveness to the idea of such a development bank – to be 'modeled on the Marshall Plan' (*New York Daily News*, 23 June 1990) – was that he had derided the initial Marshall Plan in a 1958 article as allowing the United States to gain 'control of the economies of European countries' and reduce them to 'a position analogous to that of dependencies' (Mandela, 1990, pp. 74–5). Times had changed.

Mandela also began to signal that the ANC was not wedded to its long-standing policy of nationalisation – again in direct contradiction to his statement only two months earlier that 'the nationalisation of the mines, the financial institutions and monopoly industries is the fundamental policy of the ANC and it is inconceivable that we will ever change this policy' (*Sunday Telegraph*, 1 April 1990). As if to confirm the Alliance's change of heart, Mandela (along with leading COSATU official and SACP member Chris Dlamini) had a cordial meeting with US trade union officials at the African-American Labor Center, a body previously denounced by the SACP as a front for the CIA. At the meeting, Mandela went out of his way to assure his hosts that 'state participation will not be an option if there are better options' (Trewhela, 1991, p. 79).

There were certainly many cadres in the movement who were angered by the apparent abandonment of long-held principles and policies (nowhere more so than among much of the youth and organised working class). And yet the sheer pace with which the ANC leadership was travelling down the road of accommodation and negotiation instilled in its constituency the feeling that there was little real alternative to a negotiated settlement which would entail compromise. This was further catalysed by the delegitimisation of socialist policies (associated with the collapsed economies of the USSR and Eastern Europe), and the accompanying confusion and demoralisation experienced by movement socialists.[3]

On his return to South Africa Mandela led an ANC delegation to the next round of talks. The resulting Pretoria Minute reiterated the respective parties' commitment 'to promote and expedite the normalisation and stabilisation of the situation in line with the spirit of mutual trust obtaining among the leaders involved'. It was agreed that the release of all political prisoners would be expedited no later than 30 April 1991, that security legislation would undergo continuous 'review' and that 'additional mechanisms of communication ... should be developed at local, regional, and national levels'. While these agreements represented a continuation of the efforts begun at the Groote Schuur talks, the Pretoria talks produced a completely unexpected bombshell: the ANC was to suspend the armed struggle unilaterally 'in the interest of moving as speedily as possible towards a negotiated peaceful political settlement'. With this added provision the Minute concluded that 'the way is now open to proceed towards negotiation on a new constitution' (Institute for Black Research, 1993, pp. 281–3).

This decision caused understandable confusion among MK cadres and many Alliance supporters, and the following questions were asked:

- Had the conditions, set down in the Harare Declaration for suspension of armed activities, been met by the government?
- Was not MK supposed to be the protector of the people who were under constant violent attack by the state security forces and their surrogates?
- Had the ANC leadership not continually reiterated that the armed struggle would continue until 'a democratically elected government was in power'? (*Saturday Star*, 26 May 1990).
- Above all, had not the leadership consistently promised to involve its mass base in any important decisions so that the negotiations process would not take place over the heads of the people?

For the leadership, the decision reflected a 'justified tactical compromise to maintain the momentum towards a negotiated settlement', that gave the ANC 'the moral high ground' (Barrell, 1990, pp. 69–70). Even though the leadership stressed that armed struggle would not be totally abandoned, the possibility of any return to substantive armed activity, under the conditions of a complete commitment to a 'peaceful negotiated settlement', was extremely limited. The desire to claim 'the moral high ground' gave a further indication that the ANC desired to impress upon the international community the seriousness of its 'new' approach. Unfortunately for the ANC's grassroots, questions of rectitude were hardly paramount in the face of continuing violence.

Although it had long been clear that the armed struggle would not deliver the overthrow of the apartheid state, its historic importance lay in its psychological and symbolic impact on both the apartheid state and the masses. With the suspension of the armed struggle, Alliance supporters on the ground were, more than ever, vulnerable to state-sponsored violence and dependent on an uneven negotiations process to deliver their expectations. The abandonment of organised armed activity only further contributed to the lack of direction and organisation among the mass base of the ANC. MK activity, despite its limited threat, had at least served to provide some sort of focus for the activities of the disparate groupings in the townships. Without the active presence and experience of MK cadres the people (particularly the youth) were left to their own devices, further contributing to indiscipline and anarchic behaviour (for example, youthful comrades using their ANC credentials to cover for criminal activity).

The Pretoria Minute confirmed de Klerk's control of the negotiation terrain. By giving up its armed activity and continuing to rely on exhortations to de Klerk to accede to its long-standing demands, the ANC was playing to the government's ability to dictate the pace and character of a negotiated settlement.

Not unexpectedly, the Pretoria talks were followed by an unprecedented wave of violence, centred in the Johannesburg townships, in which over 500 people died in a 10-day period (Institute for Black Research, 1993, p. 28). Attacks were directed at township residents in general, many of whom claimed no particular political allegiance and, as before, all indications pointed to the involvement of Inkhata-aligned hostel dwellers and the state security forces. In the face of such violence, many township dwellers appealed to the ANC for weapons. In the Phola Park squatter camp on the outskirts of Johannesburg, one resident made this plea:

> It will take a long time before we get the money and maybe by that time we [will] be dead and unable to enjoy the luxuries money can buy. Give us arms please. (*The Star*, 16 September 1990)

In what was to become a familiar pattern of response to the violence, the Alliance leadership pointed to a covert state-aided 'third force'[4] as being responsible, and promised to investigate the violence and take up the matter with the government. But as the violence continued MK leaders made calls for the formation of self-defence units in the townships (although MK was officially 'confined to barracks'), and the Alliance leadership adopted a more hardline attitude to the government and Inkhata. De Klerk responded by launching his own security crackdown, and although it was ostensibly directed at restoring 'peace and stability', the practical effect was further to harass, intimidate and eliminate grassroots Alliance leaders and activists. Having no other recourse, the ANC leadership announced the suspension of talks with the government.

With no real alternative to continued negotiation the ANC's decision represented both an attempt to placate its grassroots base and to put pressure on de Klerk to create a climate conducive to further negotiation. The ANC leadership had not only placed far too much trust in a strategy of talks which relied heavily on 'trust' and 'integrity', but had failed to follow its own call that the negotiations process would be led by the people. Without rooting its chosen negotiations strategy in mass mobilisation and struggle – the only other pillar of struggle which the organisation was now capable of utilising – the ANC (even if unwittingly) further contributed to de Klerk's control of the new terrain and to the organisation's strategic impotence.

The Revolutionary Zig-Zag

> If you want to safeguard your revolution you deal with the devil if necessary but you deal with the devil with a long spoon. You do it in a zigzag way. If it's necessary to get you to your target you do it.
>
> ANC NEC member Raymond Suttner
> (personal interview, November 1992)

By the time of the ANC's National Consultative Conference (14–16 December 1990) – the first 'open' conference of the ANC in almost 35 years – there was growing discontent among its supporters over the way in which the leadership had performed (*Financial Mail*, 14 December 1990). Besides the general perception that the ANC had been comprehensively outmanoeuvred in the negotiation process, Mandela's conduct on his foreign trips had dismayed many international supporters of the South African liberation movement.

Hard on the heels of his United States/Europe tour, Mandela visited Australia and Indonesia. In Australia he declared that he would not become involved with, or comment on, the Aboriginal question, thereby upsetting Aboriginal leaders, who accused him of 'hypocrisy'. Aboriginal activist Gary Foley posed a searching question: 'Why do you think he's coming out to Australia? It's not to get a better tan ... I think it's a political obscenity for him to be coming here and sucking up to all the people who wouldn't lift a finger for him while he was in jail' (*The Star*, 22 October 1990). In Indonesia, one of the world's worst human rights violators, Mandela accepted a humanitarian award and $10 million donation from the Suharto military dictatorship – and refused to speak out against the Indonesian campaign of genocide against East Timor. As in Australia he was accused of 'hypocrisy and opportunism'. A spokesperson for the East Timorese resistance movement, Front for the Liberation of East Timor (FRETILIN), summed up the feelings of those who had long supported the ANC's struggle:

> For years Mandela has asked the world to interfere in the internal affairs of South Africa. The fight for self-determination and freedom from repression in other countries is no more an 'internal matter' than apartheid in South Africa. (*Weekly Mail*, 17 May, 1991).

Against this international backdrop, the December conference revealed that internal discontent was also gathering force. Rank-and-file delegates chastised the leadership for what they saw as the soft line taken at talks with the government. Particularly harsh criticism was directed at the organisation's failure to defend its supporters adequately from violence in the townships and at the leadership's confidential and unilateral decision-making (*Weekly Mail*, 20 December 1990).

Conference delegates were clearly ambivalent about the ANC's decision to spearhead the struggle with a negotiation strategy. One resolution passed by delegates (as if in defiance of this 'new' strategic reality) declared that 'we unanimously rededicate ourselves to the four pillars of our revolutionary strategy, believing that there have been no fundamental changes in the political situation which would require a departure from our strategy'. And yet, in another resolution on negotiation, it was stated that 'conference supports and endorses the negotiations strategy outlined in the Harare Declaration' (ANC, 1990a, pp. 16–18). The delegates were thus caught in a strategic quandary. On the one hand, they were dissatisfied with a negotiations strategy which had delivered few gains, a leadership which seemed far too accommodative and an unanswered campaign of violence that had severely weakened the ANC. On the other hand, they yearned for a rejuvenated 'four pillars' strategy which would mobilise the masses and force the regime to capitulate to the majority's demands for total liberation.

Whatever the genuine desires of the delegates to put the masses at the forefront of struggle, the ANC's historic strategy of accommodation had long since made this option (including a mass-based underground and armed struggle) extremely difficult. The leadership knew that the ANC's commitment to a negotiated settlement with an apartheid capitalist state still in possession of its coercive capacity meant that the liberation movement had accepted the need for a historic compromise which did not entail a fundamental and radical transformation of 'power to the people'. However, conference delegates had yet to accept that reality – a contradiction that highlighted the historically tenuous connection between the ANC leadership's strategies and the liberatory vision of its mass base. The main battle for the ANC and its allies was now clear to everyone – seizing the negotiation initiative and gaining the moral high ground.

In an attempt to regain the initiative, the delegates passed a final resolution which instructed the leadership to 'serve notice on the regime that unless all the obstacles are removed on or before 30th April 1991, the ANC shall consider the suspension of the whole negotiations process'. It went on to declare that the ANC would 'engage in a programme of mass action ... create people's defence units ... remain committed to the strengthening and growth of the people's army MK and the underground [and that] the existing sanctions campaign should be maintained' (ANC, 1990a, pp. 18–20). The conference delegates also vigorously rejected proposals by Thabo Mbeki for the ANC to review its stance on sanctions. While the leadership had recognised that the ANC had lost control of the campaign (exemplified by the unilateral decisions by capital and several governments to drop sanctions against the de Klerk government), the uncritical way in which the entire sanctions campaign had been propagandised by the ANC harvested its own bitter fruit in the form of delegates' refusal to countenance any rethink.

While all these directives reflected the desire of delegates to reclaim the strategic initiative and strengthen the organisation, the reality of the negotiated terrain which the ANC had accepted pushed the resolutions in one direction only. That direction, as yet another conference resolution stated, was that 'the ANC's political task is to mobilise the public in mass campaigns to pressure the authorities to fulfil their tasks' (ANC, 1990a, p. 20). In other words, the ANC's negotiation-centric strategy ensured that mass struggle would serve the purpose of acting as a pressure valve on the de Klerk government to honour its end of the compromise bargain. The implications were clear:

- the ANC would accept the government as an equal partner in the search for a post-apartheid order;
- an expectant ANC would rely on more enlightened and chastened government security forces to deal with the violence;
- mass struggle, despite any alternative potential, would serve to enhance the Alliance's negotiating position (although there might be differences over degrees of emphasis).

Reflecting the tenor of the conference resolutions, the ANC NEC statement of 8 January 1991 stressed the importance of the 'mass involvement of the people in the process of negotiations'. It gave the government until 30 April to remove 'identified obstacles to the process of negotiating a new constitution', failing which, the ANC would 'review the situation'. The NEC also called for the convening of an 'all-party congress' to discuss the election of a Constituent Assembly (which in turn would draw up the constitution), and establish an 'interim government to oversee the process of transition' until a 'democratic government' was formed (ANC, 1991f).

Although the apartheid state responded positively to the NEC's call for an all-party congress, there was no indication that it was in any hurry to meet the other ANC demands. The most immediate response to the ANC's moves was the massacre (by 'unidentified men') on 12 January 1991 of 35 ANC members and supporters who were attending a funeral vigil in the township of Sebokeng on the outskirts of Johannesburg (Institute for Black Research, 1993, p. 34). The ANC leadership reacted by repeating its earlier charge that a third force existed, and once again accused the regime of not creating a climate conducive to negotiation. Even though Mandela met Inkhata leader Gatsha Buthelezi soon after the massacre and signed an agreement intended to end violence between their respective organisations, it was no more than an act of individual diplomacy and had little effect on the ground.

As the violence continued, the ANC embarked on its conference promise of mass-action campaigns. Rallies, marches and work stay-aways (mainly in the Witswatersrand and Eastern Cape regions) were held, and a signature campaign for the ANC's constituent assembly demands was undertaken. While the campaign attracted sizeable numbers, most observers, including those within the ANC, agreed that the mass action was constrained by a lack of grassroots organisation, effective communication and a general lack of direction (*Mayibuye*, March 1991). In addition, it was difficult for the masses to get excited about action aimed at affecting a negotiation process that was far removed from the more immediate local issues that had most often provided the initial impetus for their own struggles. Indeed, it was clear that the kind of mass action that did take place failed to link economic demands with larger political demands aimed at empowering the mass base.

Criticism also began to emanate from within the ANC leadership ranks This was predominantly focused on three issues: the organisation's failure to utilise mass struggle – thus contributing to ANC weakness in dealing with the government; the growing gap between the actions of the leadership and rank-and-file expectations – producing confusion over the direction of the 'struggle'; and the inability of the ANC to protect its members and supporters from violence (Kasrils and Khuzwayo, 1991; Suttner, 1991). Reflecting much the same sentiment as that expressed by delegates at the December conference, these internal critics argued that there was a need for 'a combination of mass action and negotiations' in order to regain the 'strategic initiative' (Kasrils and Khuzwayo, 1991, pp. 10–11).

Despite such perspectives, the strategic effect of the criticisms was not fundamentally to challenge the negotiation path of the ANC but rather to solidify it further. Reflecting the ANC's tradition of coopting internal debate into pre-set strategy, negotiation would now succeed – with an added emphasis on 'mass action' – where the armed struggle had failed. As an internal ANC discussion paper stated:

> Just as in the past we saw the objective of armed seizure of power as the means to effect the transition, negotiations now become a viable method for the transfer of power in the new conditions. (ANC, 1991e)

A rejuvenated campaign of mass action would no doubt give the ANC added clout at the negotiating table and potentially provide some direction and involvement for grassroots structures, but it could really only possess an inherently narrow strategic utility within the ANC's overall negotiation framework. Just as de Klerk would eventually have to rein in his security forces in order to secure legitimacy and deliver his side of the bargain, so the ANC would ultimately have to ensure that mass struggle conformed to the unspoken rules of the politics of the 'new' transition.

As the ANC's mass-action campaign lurched along and violence showed no signs of abating, the 30 April 1991 deadline for the government to meet the movement's demands loomed large. However, it was clear that the government was in no hurry to stem the violence or to convene an all-party congress. De Klerk was gaining much mileage from the perception that it was the ANC which was being obstinate over further negotiations and the characterisation of the violence as 'black-on-black' feuding between the ANC and Inkhata. At the same time it was equally clear that despite its increasingly strident threats to stop all negotiations with the government – contained in a further ultimatum issued in the ANC's 'Open Letter' to the government on 5 April, and extending the deadline to 9 May (Institute for Black Research, 1991, pp. 318–25) – the ANC had no other option but to hold out for a better deal. ANC leaders had already confirmed that negotiations were the only option (*The Star*, 11 March 1991), and soon after the radical rhetoric of the 'Open Letter' Mandela told foreign diplomats that the ANC would be 'flexible' in its ultimatum if there was 'a positive reaction' to the demands (*The Star*, 10 April 1991). The reality was that the Alliance leadership had neither the political will nor the organisational capacity – weakened considerably by its strategic approach to negotiations – to force de Klerk's hand.

On the ground the people were preoccupied with defending their communities from violent attacks. In the words of one township dweller, the Alliance's grassroots base was 'just afraid', resulting in most 'discussion centring around violence when what we need to be talking about and concentrating on is the organisation and principles of the ongoing struggle' (Simon, personal interview, October 1991).[5] Workers belonging to the most organised Alliance partner, COSATU, were also taken up with defending their communities, which severely affected their ability to direct their energies and efforts to organise around workplace demands and larger political issues. It did not help that COSATU had largely ignored the organisation and needs of migrant hostel-dwellers, which indirectly contributed to Inkhata's success in organising these alienated people to participate in violent campaigns against Alliance supporters (Ruiters and Taylor, 1990).

The ability of the liberation movement to respond adequately to the continuing violence was further hampered by the fact that the main task of the ANC's troubled armed wing, MK, had become one of preparing selected cadres for a future post-apartheid army (*Mayibuye*, April 1991, pp. 10–12). MK had attempted to involve itself in the defence of the ANC's constituency by issuing a booklet entitled *For the Sake of our Lives*, which began circulating among township activists in mid-1991. It called for the formation of Township Defence Committees and Township Defence Forces operating along military lines, adapting to the tactical needs of an urban landscape and constituting an embryonic people's army and police. While these directives were followed by MK's first full conference inside South Africa in September 1991, the conference was more notable for the intense criticism directed at ANC (and MK) leaders for unilateral decision-making and the confused state of the organisation.

As events over the next year were to confirm, MK's plans for the defence of the ANC's mass base never really gelled. While many communities did form self-defence units, they were often ill-equipped and lacked formal command and control structures. However much the MK rank and file might have been capable of, and willing to, direct the defence of the movement, the political decisions that the ANC leadership had already made left MK with little more than a spectator role.

As the grassroots fought for survival, the tug-of-war conducted on the terrain of 'on-again, off-again' negotiations process took on the quality of political theatre. For instance, throughout the first few months of 1991 the ANC had performed so many tortuous flip-flops over the Winnie Mandela trial[6] that even disinterested observers must have wondered if the organisation had completely lost its bearings. Meanwhile, in early 1991, de Klerk had left on a trip to Europe (shortly followed by Mandela) and in an ironic role-reversal it was de Klerk who was feted as the anti-apartheid hero as European governments and international capital welcomed his calls for lifting an already ailing sanctions campaign. The ANC leadership countered de Klerk's successes by claiming that 'the notion that the weakening on the sanctions front represents a defeat is a lot of nonsense – it is a reflection of the victories we are scoring' (*New Nation*, 3–9 May 1990). And yet the ANC had certainly not helped its international sanctions cause by purchasing the Shell Oil Company's flagship building in Johannesburg as home for its new administrative headquarters – Shell continued to be a main target of the international anti-apartheid movement (*New African*, 21 February 1991).

During this period, Alliance leaders were desperately trying to project their organisation as being in control of the negotiations process. While telling grassroots supporters to prepare for mass protest and general strikes (*The Star*, 30 April 1991), they were also telling international capital that a negotiated deal was imminent. Thabo Mbeki went so far as virtually to dismiss the existence of any substantive obstacles to concluding a deal when he told leading businessmen at a conference held in Zimbabwe that the ANC saw 'no particular reason why there should not be a new constitution in South Africa by the end of this year' (*The Star*, 24 April 1991). Indeed, the conflicting statements even extended to the issue of violence. In 1990, not a month after his organisation had heaped all sorts of vitriol on de Klerk for being responsible for the violence, Mbeki projected the State President as a man committed to a 'non-racial ... democratic' South Africa, under siege from a hostile white right (*New Nation*, 3–9 May 1990). It was no wonder that the ANC was losing the battle for the strategic initiative to de Klerk.

Damn the Torpedoes, Full Speed Ahead

The ANC held its 48th National Congress in Durban on 2–7 July 1991. Over 2000 delegates listened as Mandela opened the conference with an exhortation to prepare for negotiations 'sooner rather than later'. Accusing the de Klerk government of pursuing a 'double agenda', Mandela urged the conference to ensure that ANC strategy and policy would 'push the process forward leading to the transfer of power [for] our people' (ANC, 1991b). Over the next several days delegates engaged in open and often intense debate. Outgoing ANC Secretary-General, Alfred Nzo, produced a scathing report on the state of the organisation, painting a picture of a 'reactive' ANC riddled with complacency, confusion and lack of initiative, and confined by 'populist rhetoric and clichés' (*The Star*, 7 July 1991).

While it may have sounded as though the ANC was being chastised for being out of touch with its mass constituency, Nzo (himself not very popular with the rank and file) was a conduit for a different kind of message from the leadership. That message was simply that the ANC leadership wanted the membership to accept the strategic reality of the new negotiated transition: in other words, the leadership expected the rank and file to jettison any revolutionary expectations and activities.

Elections at the Congress produced only one real surprise, that of former National Union of Mineworkers head, Cyril Ramaphosa, as Secretary-General. His election had not been expected since he was relatively young and had not been in exile. Filling the other major positions were Nelson Mandela (President-General) and Walter Sisulu (Deputy-President). However, the new-look, 50-member NEC contained many former UDF leaders; as did the more streamlined 27-member National Working Committee (NWC), which was given the task of overseeing the running of the organisation on a full-time basis.

While the SACP had begun to assert itself as an independent organisation outside the ANC (for example, opening new SACP branches and recruiting heavily among trade unions), the role its members played at the Congress was consistent with past practice: putting forward a left version of the national democratic revolution yet remaining solidly within the strategic parameters of the ANC's united-front approach. Indeed, it was the reaffirmation of a united-front perspective, reflected in the strategic synthesis of the final resolutions, that signified the most important result of the Congress. Although the resolutions covered a complex array of issues that had previously been given little attention (for example, countering state propaganda and increasing the role of women within the organisation), the main thrust was to commit the ANC unreservedly to a negotiated settlement. Reiterating much of what had come out of the December conference, the resolutions directed the NEC to implement a programme of action to remove all obstacles to negotiations (with special emphasis on violence), and to 'draw in as many categories of people and organisations behind the broad goals of non-racialism, non-sexism and democracy' (ANC, 1991b).

The proceedings also highlighted the extent to which the ANC was dependent on foreign funding, particularly from Sweden. Although the official figures were not released, one source put the amount pledged by foreign sources by the end of 1991 at R684 million. While it remained to be seen whether these pledges would be realised, the ANC could count on receiving a reported R54 million from the Swedish International Development Agency – a figure that represented a substantial percentage of the ANC's budget (Institute for Black Research, 1991, p. 38).

While the Congress succeeded in pulling together the various strands of the ANC behind the chosen negotiation strategy, there was nothing particularly new about what came out of Durban. What the first Congress on home territory in three decades represented was the formal return of the ANC to its historical strategic mission – bringing together the broadest social coalition to put pressure on the state to negotiate the terms of apartheid's demise. Despite the ANC's consistent claims that such a strategy would deliver a genuine 'transfer of power to the people', the ANC's battle plan after almost 80 years of existence looked more like the terms for a gentleman's agreement.

One of the more immediate results of the Congress was the ANC's attempt to project itself as an all-inclusive organisation by propagandising a non-ideological image. Mandela, echoing Mbeki's earlier statements, argued that:

[the ANC is] united solely by our determination to oppose racial oppression ... [it] is the only thing that unites us ... there is no question of ideology as far as the odyssey of the ANC is concerned, because any question approaching ideology would split the organisation from top to bottom. (Sparks, 1991, p. 8)

Just like the UDF in the 1980s, the ANC was attempting to present its broad alliance programme as possessing no specific ideological content. Just as the UDF's attempt had been disingenuous, so too was this.

The ANC was attempting to separate cause from effect. The fact that a general anti-apartheidism was seen as the glue for organisational viability did not mean that the way in which apartheid was to be removed was devoid of specific ideological considerations. As an example, the ANC's decision to pursue a broad alliance, inclusive of domestic and international monopoly capitalism under the historic conditions pertaining in South Africa, was not merely a short-term tactical move, but a strategic choice rooted in a specific conception of class power. Similarly the ANC's preference for a mixed-economy solution (part state-led, part private sector-led) to the ravages of apartheid capitalism entailed ideological choices relating to class benefits and empowerment.

The conception of class power that the majority petit-bourgeois leadership of the ANC possessed was one of aspiration; that is, it was defined by that class they aspired to join – the bourgeoisie. Instead of seeing the radical possibilities of the struggles of the broad mass, they saw the political and economic power of the ruling class (state and capital). Thus the defining logic of the leadership's struggle for national liberation was cast as one of accession and aspiration, all within the boundaries of a racialised conception of change.

The logic of the supposedly non-ideological approach of the ANC was clearly revealed by Zola Skweyiya of the ANC's Legal Department (now Minister of Public Services). He argued that:

> Entrenching the mixed economy in the constitution will provide opportunities for *maintaining and consolidating* the unity of the anti-apartheid forces which has been forged in the anti-apartheid struggle and channel it to the task of national and economic development. (*Sechaba*, June 1989, p. 9; emphasis added)

Thus the broad alliance against apartheid was not to be a temporary one, but one that would be maintained and consolidated after liberation. Indeed, the entire strategic trajectory of a negotiated settlement was wrapped in layers of ideological and class considerations.

Not long after the Durban Congress, the ANC was given a short-lived boost in its tug-of-war with the de Klerk government by revelations that government security forces had diverted state funds to the Inkhata movement (*Weekly Mail*, 19 July 1991). 'Inkhatagate', as it came to be known, forced de Klerk to admit the funding and demote (to lesser government positions) long-time securocrats Magnus Malan and Adriaan Vlok (Ministers of Defence and Law and Order respectively). Yet for all the sensationalism surrounding the revelations and the undeniable link between the government and Inkhata against the ANC, neither de Klerk nor Buthelezi suffered much more than temporary damage. The violence did not significantly diminish and the signing of a National Peace Accord between de Klerk, Mandela and Buthelezi in September 1991 did little to stem the slaughter. Ironically, de Klerk was able to consolidate further his control of the National Party now that Malan and Vlok had been substantially marginalised.

Indeed it was a mark of de Klerk's confidence and continued ability to set the pace and character of the transition process – and conversely the ANC's inability to set the transitional agenda – that resulted in his giving the nod for the unilateral imposition of a new, anti-progressive, across-the-board Value Added Tax (VAT) in late

1991. The effects of this tax would mostly be felt by a black populace already heavily burdened by the crisis of apartheid capitalism. Indeed, the South African economy had registered negative growth in 1991, and unemployment was (unofficially) hovering at around 40 per cent. In addition, there had been large-scale retrenchments and increasing monopolisation of industry as capital continually sought to mitigate the effects of its continuing crisis.

De Klerk's imposition of VAT proved a wake-up call for the ANC's Alliance partner COSATU. Since February 1990, COSATU's profile in the Alliance had been low, partly as a result of independent working-class action being severely curtailed by the violence, but also because of COSATU's approach to mass struggle. Following the same general negotiation strategy as the ANC, COSATU had become involved in a parallel negotiating process with capital and the state. After signing accords with the state and domestic capital – providing for its participation in the state's National Manpower Commission – COSATU devoted much of its energies to institutionalising bargaining agreements between unions, employers and the state.

One result of this was to curtail mass struggle by the organised working class. Although COSATU leaders (like ANC leaders) continued to stress that their negotiations process was in the interests of their constituency and needed to be mass-led, the reality was that workers often had little say in decisions made in the 'tripartite' forums. The perceived necessity of seeking common ground with capital and the state for some kind of social contract in the drive to restructure (albeit on a more progressive bent) an ailing South African capitalism meant that mass struggle by the working class would need to be contained within the parameters of that very negotiating process. Within the broader strategic framework of political negotiation involving their political representatives, the ANC and SACP, working-class demands and struggle would of necessity have to be muted in order for the 'deal' to be delivered.

A classic example of this involved the issue of nationalisation. While most workers continued to demand nationalisation (particularly of monopoly capital) as a means towards socialisation of the means of production (COSATU, 1992), ANC leaders were busy trying to convince their broad alliance that nationalisation was no longer 'an ideological attachment' of the organisation (*The Star*, 17 September 1991).[7] In fact, it had been clear since early 1990 that the ANC leadership saw nationalisation as a stone around their neck in their bid to secure foreign investment and the support of liberal capital. Likewise, the ANC had decided that it would not nationalise private land for redistribution to the people, but rather use vacant and unused land (including state-owned properties such as military installations) as well as a Land Claims Court to fulfil the Freedom Charter's promise that 'the land shall be shared among those who work it' (ANC, 1991a).

Once VAT had been imposed by the state, COSATU mobilised an anti-VAT coalition and called a two-day nationwide strike in protest. The strike, the largest in South African history, succeeded in virtually shutting down the economy. Despite this impressive display of power by organised workers, VAT was not rescinded and high-level talks resumed centre-stage. The result indicated that as long as mass struggle continued to be strategically confined within a necessarily accommodationist negotiation process, the interests of workers and the broad mass of people would take a back seat to those of capital and a state intent on preserving as much of the economic status quo as possible.

Delivering the Deal

As the end of 1991 approached, the ANC and the government were making preparations for the convening of an all-party congress. While the ANC could claim that the government had acceded in principle to some of its long-standing demands, such as the need for an Interim Government of National Unity (IGNU), the (supposed) disbanding of covert operations and the repealing of race laws, the truth was that the government had done so on terms and in a time-frame it had largely determined. Despite conferences, endless policy positions, recognition of the agenda of the government and capital and undeniable popular support, the ANC leadership and that of its Alliance partners had been comprehensively outplayed by the de Klerk government. As the South Africa correspondent of the UK *Independent*, John Carlin, pointed out:

> Mr. Mandela, and the other 'moderates' in the ANC leadership took Mr. de Klerk at face value. They believed that the government and the ANC would be equal partners in the voyage to the 'New South Africa,' that apartheid would go and they, as the natural majority party, would glide into power ... In one sense [that] trust was not misplaced. Mr. de Klerk will remove apartheid from the statute books. He will, when it suits him, release the political prisoners. But this was never the issue; he knew from the day he came to power that this was what had to be done. The real issue was to retain power, to perpetuate white privilege and the economic status quo after apartheid had gone. (*Independent*, 24 April 1991)

On the specific issue of the release of all political prisoners (a demand of the Harare Declaration), the ANC leadership had continuously referred to such releases as necessary to creating a 'climate conducive to negotiations'. And yet there were still many political prisoners languishing in jail, particularly those who were aligned to the ANC. Despite numerous pleas and letters to the leadership from ANC-aligned political prisoners (particularly from a group in Leuwkop Maximum Security Prison),[8] there continued to be little movement on the issue throughout 1992 and 1993. Although the ANC and the apartheid state had signed a Record of Understanding in September 1992 designed to release all genuine political prisoners, the ultimate power to decide still rested with de Klerk. Meanwhile, the regime continued to release prisoners aligned to Inkhata yet stalled on taking any action with regards to ANC-aligned prisoners. As for the ANC leadership, it consistently resorted to telling the prisoners to wait until a new government was in place.

The Convention for a Democratic South Africa (CODESA), constituted as the formal gathering of an all-party congress, got underway in late December 1991. As proceedings began, it was more obvious than ever that the ANC and the SACP were determined to wrap up the negotiation process as soon as possible. Mandela now spoke of the need to 'develop consensus across the spectrum and of the desire to maximize common purpose amongst South Africans' (Institute for Black Research, 1991, p. 56). The SACP, fresh from its eighth national congress, declared that negotiations were the 'shortest and most peaceful route to the transfer of power to the people'. Following the adoption of its two-stage theory to the 'new' conditions, the SACP continued to insist that if the 'working class propels this process' (that is, negotiation) the process would not 'fail the working class' (SACP, 1992, p. 11). It seemed as if the SACP leadership saw no contradiction between the negotiation strategy and its necessarily accommodative politics, and the ability of the working class to struggle for socialism.

Although there was a great deal of political posturing between the ANC leadership and the apartheid state at the new talks, the proceedings, which continued into late May 1992, clearly indicated that the ANC was prepared to be increasingly flexible in its desire to implement a 'transfer of power to the people'. Everything became negotiable, including protection for minorities, highly decentralised federalism, immediate reincorporation of the 'homelands', as well as majority rule (at least for the short term). In addition to the myriad policy U-turns since February 1990, including those on nationalisation and land, the ANC was now ready to:

- welcome international capital and Western government involvement in creating a 'democratic' economy (*The Star*, 6 December 1991), including a tentative endorsement of

IMF and World Bank prescriptions on macro-economic policy (*Business Day*, 24 March 1992);
- categorically rule out armed struggle as an alternative to a negotiated settlement (*The Star*, 20 May 1992);
- accept an interim constitution and interim government negotiated within the confines of CODESA (ANC, 1992b, p. 9).

All of this took place against the background of continuing violence, limited mass action and an increasingly confident National Party, aided by its victory in the March 1992 all-white referendum on negotiations. Indeed, de Klerk had managed to:

- tie up the ANC in months of talks in which the government had conceded little;
- get the Alliance to back an all-white referendum which enhanced the NP's position and helped create the impression that the real enemy of 'peace and democracy' was the white right;
- keep overall control of the state machinery;
- consistently side-step responsibility for a campaign of violence that weakened the ANC.

In an indication of de Klerk's stubborn 'success', the CODESA talks broke down at the end of May, ostensibly over percentages for the approval of decisions to be taken by a future constitution-making body. For its part, the ANC negotiators, in their search for consensus, offered a 70 per cent majority for approval while government negotiators stuck arrogantly to a figure of 80 per cent. The real reason for the deadlock, however, lay with the Alliance leadership's belated realisation that its increasingly alienated mass base needed to be reassured that it was not being sold a half-baked liberation.

Soon after the deadlock at CODESA the ANC held a National Policy Conference at which delegates decided to issue the apartheid state with yet another ultimatum. It encompassed most previous demands (for example, on violence and political prisoners) but was very specific on the installation of an Interim Government of National Unity (to be agreed upon by the end of June 1992), and on a freely elected constitution-making body (by the end of the year). ANC Secretary-General Cyril Ramaphosa warned the government that there had to be 'firm timetables' and that if the demands were not met, the Alliance would embark on 'unprecedented mass action' (*The Star*, 1 June 1992). As had been the case in the past, the apartheid state seemed intent on ignoring the immediate demands of the Alliance, preferring to sit tight and wait on more secret high-level meetings to get formal negotiation back on track.

However, on the night of 17 June 1992 hostel dwellers descended on the squatter settlement of Boipatong (on the outskirts of Johannesburg) and slaughtered 45 people, wounding many more. There was an immediate outpouring of domestic and international outrage and ANC supporters demanded that the organisation take action against a regime they had consistently held responsible for the violence. Mandela was told by angry Boipatong residents that the Alliance leadership was 'acting like lambs while the enemy is killing our people' (*The Star*, 28 June 1992). It was a familiar refrain, and the Alliance leadership knew that it would have to give its mass base some indication of support. An announcement soon followed that the Alliance was suspending all talks with the government.

Activities and events over the next three months, despite opportunities for substantively shifting the balance of forces in favour of the ANC's mass base, served to confirm the strategic stranglehold of an accommodative negotiation path. The Alliance began a 'rolling mass action' campaign designed to 'politically defeat de Klerk', and to ensure that the 'people are part of the process of deciding their own futures' (*The Star*, 12 July 1992). Alliance leaders such as Ronnie Kasrils, who had shown some unease about the negotiations process, saw in the campaign the insurrectionary 'possibility of the Leipzig option'[9] in which 'we reach the stage where de Klerk is propelled out of the exit gate' (*Weekly Mail*, 19 June 1992). Such sentiments, while understandable given the lack of mass mobilisation and involvement since 1990, soon gave way to the harsh reality that Alliance leaders continued to see mass struggle as a pressure tactic on a negotiation process to which they were completely committed.

The *Sowetan* newspaper (South Africa's largest 'black' daily paper) reported Cyril Ramaphosa as telling Alliance members that the ANC had 'precipitated the talks deadlock ... so our people could see we are dealing with an enemy that will not give in easily'. He was also quoted as saying that 'there is no alternative' to CODESA (*Sowetan*, 6 July 1992). Soon afterwards, the ANC leadership reiterated its commitment to negotiations and reassured the country that its mass-action campaign 'is not a programme of insurrection' aimed at 'a forceful overthrow' (*Weekly Mail*, 16 July 1992).

The subsequent campaign of 'rolling mass action', despite high expectations from Alliance supporters and dire warnings of 'crisis' and 'chaos' from the apartheid state and capital, bore the stamp of muted pressure. As one activist put it:

> The weakness in the way the involvement of the masses in negotiations has been posed is that it has focused almost

exclusively on the process of *consultation and symbolic or demonstrative actions.* (Tumahole, 1993; original emphasis)

A nationwide general strike in August (the planned culmination of the campaign), which had originally been set to last an entire week and which many militant workers had argued should be open-ended, was reduced to a two-day work stay-away after leaders of the Alliance and representatives of monopoly capital reached a compromise in closed talks. While the strike and accompanying rallies and marches showed that the Alliance had the capacity to mobilise its militant mass base for specific activities, they clearly confirmed the primacy of a bounded strategic approach to mass struggle and a dominant politics of accommodation.

Nowhere was this more clearly revealed than in the aftermath of the 7 September 1992 Bisho massacre in the Ciskei homeland. Ciskei security forces (commanded by white officers from the South African Defence Force) opened fire on an Alliance march, killing 29 people (Institute for Black Research, 1993, p. 107). Seething after yet another example of what they saw as the state's double agenda, Alliance supporters made calls for the complete abandonment of negotiations and de Klerk warned of civil war. Mandela went on national television to call for 'calm' and after talking with de Klerk – who offered to move forward on the ANC's demands on hostels, political prisoners and the carrying of dangerous weapons – declared in a highly publicised newspaper interview that the ANC was 'ready to co-operate'. Mandela further warned of a country on the brink of 'disaster', in which angry youth despised 'anything that relates to order' and 'any attitudes of hostility or action which will further damage the economy' must be avoided. He apologised for 'errors committed' during the Bisho march and presented mass action as 'a peaceful form of channelling the anger of our people', reassuring doubters that 'we are not challenging here, not demanding' (*The Star*, 15 September 1992) .

Less than two weeks later, on 28 September 1992, Mandela and de Klerk signed an Accord of Understanding. The National Party government agreed on the need for an Interim Government of National Unity (IGNU) to be installed within a specified time-frame, to take actions to secure hostels, ban the carrying of dangerous weapons in public and free all political prisoners within ten days. In return, the ANC undertook to review its mass action campaign and re-enter multi-party talks. The government had yet again conceded little. The specifics of an IGNU would still have to negotiated and the other undertakings had all been promised before (as it had always turned out, the promises were not kept). For its part, the Alliance leadership felt the need to offer further compromises in order to ensure the irreversibility of the negotiation process and to deliver the oft-stated need for 'peace and democracy'.

In a repetition of what had taken place in the 1960s and 1980s, the ANC NEC adopted a 'Strategic Perspectives' document which mirrored the suggestions made in a recent contribution by SACP negotiator Joe Slovo. In an article in the *African Communist* (1992) entitled 'Negotiations: What Room for Compromise?', Slovo argued that the 'balance of forces', in which the apartheid state was not 'a defeated enemy' and 'a revolutionary seizure of power' had not occurred, necessitated 'compromises' in order to 'create the possibility of a major positive breakthrough'. Terming the proposed scenario as one of a 'sunset clause', Slovo argued that the Alliance should agree to a time-limited power-sharing deal with de Klerk's regime (Slovo, 1992).

Although there ensued heated debate among Alliance intellectuals and activists over Slovo's proposals,[10] the NEC's 'Strategic Perspectives' document (issued in late November) left no doubt that the ANC was prepared to share power with de Klerk and his Nationalist Party cronies. As an internal ANC paper stated, 'we need to be very honest with our members ... what the NEC is advocating for a transitional period is not the same as conventional majority rule' (Suttner, 1993). None the less, the NEC continued to insist that even this ultimate of compromises did not fundamentally alter the historic strategic mission of the ANC. The 'Strategic Perspectives' document argued that:

> The strategic perspective of the ANC is the transfer of power from the white minority regime to the people as a whole. This will usher in a new era characterised by the complete eradication of the system of apartheid, fundamental socio-economic transformation, peace and stability for all our people. The basic principle underpinning this new order is democratic majority rule. (ANC, 1992c, p. 348)

While much of the Alliance's mass base remained understandably confused over this latest of contradictory messages, one thing was apparent: the Alliance, in conjunction with capital and the apartheid state, would now be able to conclude the oft-disrupted march to a deracialised capitalism in a 'new' South Africa offering something for everybody.

Whatever transpired in the resumed private meetings and negotiation after the ANC's offer of power-sharing would now be concerned with working out technicalities, trying to bring on board recalcitrant parties and sidelining, if necessary, those expressing opposition. The deal had been delivered.

Conclusion

Old Wine in New Bottles

As had been the case in previous years, 1993 proved to be a study in how to pursue the idea of national unity at almost any cost. While the by now commonplace political violence and arrogant power-plays of the de Klerk regime continued, the ANC leadership displayed a consistent preoccupation with what were perceived as serious threats to the transition coming from the far right.[1] In its annual statement, the ANC NEC highlighted the rationale for further compromise by pointing to the need to 'neutralise dangerous opposition and ... assist in curbing counter-revolution' (ANC, 1993). Strategically, this meant the prioritisation of a negotiated terrain of struggle which would gain a measure of democracy, limited by the objective conditions under which it was being pursued. This process, it was hoped, would then be radically transformed after the ANC was in power.

The sense that, once the ANC had come to possess a degree of power, major problem areas (for example, monopoly control of the economy) would be addressed and sorted out came to represent the 'official' response to the so-viewed unrealistic expectations of the organisation's mass base. The ANC leadership now argued that it was impossible to confront such problems at the present; to do so would endanger the negotiations process. Put another way, the very demands that had driven South Africa's struggle for liberation and around which the vast majority of the 'people's' struggles had coalesced, were no longer viewed as necessary to achieve the (more immediate) transformation of South Africa. Like the ANC's approach to the possibilities of a right-wing counter-revolution, this was predicated on a one-sided strategic interpretation of the prevailing socioeconomic and political conditions.

As this book has argued, this kind of perspective is infused with a petit-bourgeois politics which privileges the power of the dominant class (inclusive of the existing state) over the power of the broad mass in the struggle for liberation. This thus leads to the struggles of the people being viewed as *ad hoc* requirements to a more important, instrumentalist structural access to power (that is, control of the form not the content). The same kind of perspective has been dominant among the leadership of many national liberation movements.[2] Indeed, the global landscape of post-independence political practice by these movements only confirms the triumph of the narrow sureties of structural access to power over the fluid possibilities of popular struggle. It then becomes clear why the ANC's strategic conduct of the liberation struggle (despite all the favourable elements for a more radically transformative outcome) came to represent the effective separation of political leadership and organisation from the people.

Implicit in such a perspective is a completely undialectical approach to the ways in which political struggle is conducted. Despite the ANC's stated recognition of the need for a dialectical approach to struggle,[3] the practical politics of the ANC served seriously to undermine the possibilities of people's victories which might have propelled the dialectic in a radically different direction. It is as if both the compromises themselves and the grassroots struggles of the majority had no effect beyond their immediate transitional context, and that future possibilities were not linked to present and ongoing political (strategic) choices. Looking at the broader historical framework of the ANC's liberation struggle in which this perspective was regularly applied, it becomes clear why a gradual disempowerment of the masses emerged and ultimately an increasingly truncated liberation. To this end, the ANC leadership continued to prioritise *in camera* talks in the hope that further deals and guarantees would safeguard the stated aim of a transition to 'national democracy'.

The insistence on placing the strategic centre of struggle squarely within the parameters of an ultimately narrow and elite-managed political process of negotiation catalysed a growing frustration which was being felt by many of the ANC-led Alliance's own mass constituency. Writing in the pages of the ANC mouthpiece *Mayibuye* in April 1993, an 'ordinary' ANC member posed a searching question:

> It seems fitting to ask: Are we going to increasingly see the ANC beat one retreat after another in the face of the intransigence of the extreme right, and, indeed, of the NP itself? The position adopted by the NEC of the ANC ... points in the direction of a chain of retreats, although they might be sugared by some rhetoric of victory.

It was while such sentiments were being openly expressed by the movement's rank and file that the immensely popular leader of the SACP, Chris Hani, was gunned down by a right-wing assassin in April 1993. The resultant outpouring of anger and frustration by millions of workers and unemployed provided the Alliance leadership with a tragic but welcome weapon which they could wield in the negotiation-centric battle for moral supremacy. Once again, though, the leadership channelled the actual and potential militancy of the Alliance's base constituency into stage-managed mass action.

This took the form of tightly controlled marches and rallies in which the leadership continuously stressed the need for people to remain calm and to show maturity in the face of the incessant violence of the police and army. For instance, when thousands of youths and workers took to the streets in an outpouring of anger soon after Hani's death, their violent confrontations with the apartheid security forces were condemned as unruly behaviour which would hamper the compromise-seeking efforts of the leadership. It was as if the leadership had returned to the 1950s and were demanding that movement supporters act as though the intervening 35 years were now a distant memory. This does not imply that there was no need for disciplined struggle; however, the way in which the Alliance leadership perceived such discipline turned the positive dialectic of revolutionary struggle on its head. Instead of seeing and believing in the possibilities of active mass struggle to undermine the power of both the apartheid state and capital through the parallel expression of people's power, the approach of the Alliance substantively undermined its radical potentialities.

In spite of this it was through such channelling that the Alliance leadership was able to brandish the threat of this militancy, like the sword of Damocles, over the head of de Klerk and the white population in general. In doing so it sought at least three specific outcomes:

- to pressure de Klerk to make good his promises of meeting the ANC's basic demands which it had set down in 1990;
- to frighten intransigent whites (particularly in the business sector) into accepting the ANC as the best guarantor of peace and stability;
- to control the militancy within the movement that itself posed a potential threat to the strategic centrality of accommodative negotiation.

On all three objectives there was enough success to ensure the solidification of the Alliance's chosen strategic path: an all-inclusive negotiated settlement culminating in national elections for a government of national unity. Unquestionably though, the price of such unity was high.

Searching for Unity in the Face of Contradiction

For three decades the dominant theoretical basis for the ANC's liberation struggle had been cast within the necessity for the revolutionary seizure of power. Whether applied to the smashing of apartheid and the attainment of majority rule or as a springboard to a transition to socialism, the revolutionary seizure of power was presented as a necessary precondition for movement forward. Years earlier, Joe Slovo had put it this way:

> Thus there is a distinction between the creation of the new state form and the building of a new socialist economic formation. The former is made possible by a revolutionary seizure of power; the latter, through the exercise of that political power by a class whose interests are unconditionally served by a socialist order. (Slovo, 1976, pp. 146–7)

Historically, many liberal and neo-Marxist academics, as well as numerous Alliance intellectuals, have conceptualised arguments for a revolutionary seizure of power in narrowly statist terms. As a result, the (autonomous) state is given the status of the struggle 'throne', leaving revolutionary (purposive) struggle cast in terms of a fight for a specific form (structure) of power rather than its foundation. If such an approach is adopted, either theoretically or practically, a false dichotomy emerges between the political and the economic 'sides' of revolutionary struggle. Thus political control of the state can be achieved with no corresponding transformation of the economic sphere; we only have to take one quick glance at the contemporary results of most third world political revolutions to see what kind of national liberation has been delivered. In the historical context of the South African struggle such approaches have provided the basis from which to lend both revolutionary credence to purely political change and ammunition for bourgeois critics of any revolutionary struggle.

There is nothing implicitly statist in any struggle for revolutionary change. What is implicit, though, is that there must be a fundamental attack on the entrenched economic and political interests of capital (in whatever form) in order for there to be meaningful liberation. As the ANC had put this quite clearly in the 1970s:

> It is therefore a fundamental feature of our strategy that victory must embrace more than formal political democracy. To allow the existing economic forces to retain their interests intact is to feed the root of racial supremacy and does not represent even a shadow of liberation. (Slovo, 1976, p. 111)

And yet the cumulative effect of the strategic and tactical programme of the ANC, consummated in the post-1990 transitional period, has been gradually to demobilise the only constituency capable of leading and carrying through such a revolutionary struggle – that class of South Africa's workers and unemployed. The strategic primacy given to the achievement of a narrowly conceived national democracy has allowed a fundamental contradiction to permeate the South African liberation struggle: in the liberation struggle the ANC's own base constituency have ultimately had to be fellow-travellers with a whole host of powerful social forces whose fundamental interests are inimical to revolutionary transformation.

From a peculiarly romanticised attachment to classic guerrilla warfare, to a rhetorically heavy notion of insurrectionary people's power, to social and political contracts with capital, the strategic thrust of the ANC's struggle for national liberation has consistently underestimated and seriously undermined the potential and actual struggle of the people themselves. More specifically, the political strategies of the liberation movement have led to a lack of recognition and incorporation of actual struggles on the ground.

What has made this cumulative strategy all the more removed from the possibilities of attaining a genuine transfer of power to the people has been the false separation, both theoretical and practical, between political and socioeconomic change. For this reason, processes such as democratisation have taken on a narrow petit-bourgeois, nationalist and predominantly political meaning and context. With such an approach there can be no real analytical or strategic distinction between national liberation struggles and socialist revolution. This perspective is thus left with no other option than to see socioeconomic change as secondary to the parallel struggle for political change (that is, it privileges the economic status quo – capitalism).

It is not surprising then that many movement leaders and intellectuals have claimed that the political changes brought about after the April 1994 elections (even if initially in the form of temporary co-governance with the National Party) have laid the foundation for fundamental social and economic change.[4] Indeed, the Alliance's Reconstruction and Development Programme (RDP)[5] is pointed to as an example of ongoing policy formation that can deliver, at the very least, basic material needs to the people. And yet if analysed in the general context of the ANC's strategic path (both past and present), it is not difficult to see that the potentialities of the RDP are inherently bounded by the very same logic and practice that infused previous phases of liberation struggle. Indeed, since April 1994 the ANC-led government has managed to turn the RDP into another tool of consensus politics, and in the process ditch its radical potential in favour of a more 'realistic' free-market political economy that has little to offer South Africa's workers and the poor.[6]

A major contradiction that has permeated ANC politics is the unwillingness and/or inability to recognise that revolutionary struggle cannot be advanced by attempting to reconcile the priorities of the people with the priorities of capital. Indeed, the same critique can be applied to many of the national liberation movements of the last 30 years. What makes a critical appraisal of the ANC's liberation struggle so important though is the enduring (mis)perception that the character of the South African liberation struggle supersedes such contradictions. It is time this bubble was burst.

The macro-nationalist approach to struggle that has characterised Alliance politics to date has virtually institutionalised this contradiction. This approach has led to the subordination of class organisation and politics. In turn, it has allowed the struggle for liberation to be infused by, and to accept, all those 'antithetical forms of social unity' under capitalism (Marx, 1973, p. 159). In these circumstances the mass struggles for revolutionary nationalist transformation are turned into little more than a struggle for petit-bourgeois reformism. As Lenin argued in response to the economists of his day who wanted to divide political and economic struggles, the purpose of all revolutionary struggle is to integrate the two under revolutionary working-class leadership (Lenin, 1969, pp. 54–65). Only then can the rich possibilities for fundamental transformation in society be realised.

Indeed, since April 1994, the ANC leadership has shown clearly its petit-bourgeois pedigree. Constantly prioritising the search for false unity between antagonistic class and social forces, it has managed to achieve, in less than three years, what it took most other post-independence liberation movements over a decade to accomplish. It has used its newly acquired political power to:

- substantively demobilise (and/or demoralise) much of its mass base;
- provide the foundation for the accumulative needs of a (corrupt) new elite;
- pave the way for international capital to exercise increased imperialist influence and control over the economic, cultural and social life of the country;
- reinforce class, racial and gender inequality.

True to its past, the ANC leadership has rationalised all of this in terms of the need to build 'national unity' and to be 'pragmatic' and above all, by reference to the lack of any 'alternative'. In simple terms, the ANC has been trying to have its cake and eat it.

The Distorted Dialectics of Struggle

Soon after signing the Declaration of Intent with President de Klerk at the beginning of 1993, Nelson Mandela wondered out loud:

> Who would have thought that as a result of these discussions, the State of Emergency would be lifted, political prisoners released, exiles allowed to return, a climate of free political activity in the greater part of South Africa would prevail, and repressive legislation would either be amended or repealed ... [providing] a basis for movement towards a united, non-racial, democratic and non-sexist South Africa? (*Mayibuye*, February 1993, p. 9)

Unfortunately, there was no one immediately to answer his implicitly leading question. However, it could well be imagined that the response from a majority of South Africans would have been to wonder whether the 'result' of the 'discussions' (negotiations) represented a solid basis for movement towards a revolutionary and fundamental transformation of South Africa. Indeed, Mandela's thoughts encapsulate one of the central contradictions inherent in the dialectic of struggle which this book has attempted to grasp: that the ANC has historically given excessive, and often misdirected, strategic weight to the objective conditions (balance of forces) under which they have pursued the (subjective) goals and aspirations of national liberation.

Through a critical historical analysis of the ANC's struggle for national liberation in South Africa, this book has argued that the way in which this dialectic of struggle has been realised has substantively undermined the possibility for a genuinely transformative liberation. At the heart of this historic contradiction in the South African context (and applicable to many other twentieth-century liberation struggles) has been the failure strategically to prioritise the will and leading role of the base constituency within the liberation movement. Simply put, the ANC, guided by its leading members, has been unwilling to trust the very people it claims to represent; it has, in effect, been unable to trust real democracy.

By way of explanation, it is important to delineate the meaning of democracy which has become such a commonplace term that it is now used to describe anything short of fascism. At its most basic, democracy is a set of social, economic and political relationships in which the broad mass of people take control of their own lives. Placed within the context of institutionalised capitalist class power it then implies the need for oppressed classes to shape the content of democratic society (and not merely to participate in its various forms). There surely can be no predetermined conceptualisation or practice of democracy given the present uneven capacities for exercising power, under conditions where access to, and possession of, capital is a means of political and economic class control (McKinley, 1994, pp. 44–65).

In South Africa there can be little argument that the broad mass of people are the workers and unemployed, both urban and rural (and predominantly black). And yet the cumulative history of ANC practice reveals a weighted strategic tendency to emasculate the self-activity and self-emancipation of that base constituency. The dialectical relationship between the objective balance of forces in a given social milieu and the activity of those seeking to liberate themselves and fundamentally alter that balance is part of a fluid social process in which there are no absolutes nor impenetrable barriers. While the structural characteristics of apartheid capitalism have necessarily shaped the strategic approach of the ANC, the potential to transform that structure rests squarely with the struggles of the broad mass.

This book has thus applied a framework of analysis which views the structural conditions and the activities of those who are attempting to change those conditions as expressions of the political and socioeconomic reality of apartheid and capitalism; in other words, a lens for viewing the dialectic of the South African revolution. By showing the interrelatedness of elements that constitute a revolutionary theory and practice (for example, the state, imperialism and class struggle) this book avoids the trap into which other studies of revolution have fallen; that is, attempting to isolate a singular referential point to analyse and explain revolutionary periods and revolutionary action. Whether it is a state-centric, structuralist interpretation or one based on a purely subjective, organisational/value competition, unilinear theories of revolution end up atomising the complexities of revolution itself.

What this book has tried to make clear is that the struggle for the liberation of South Africa, as practised by the ANC, has failed to place the revolutionary struggles of the oppressed at the centre of its revolutionary practice and to locate itself firmly within the broad mass as a means to the desired end – liberation for a full transfer of power to the people. Until such time, the majority of South Africans, who continue to suffer under the ravages of capitalism in whatever 'new' international or national form, will continue struggling to realise a truly new vision of society – *a luta continua!*

Notes

Preface

1. See in particular V.I. Lenin, 'What is to be Done?' and 'The Proletarian Revolution and Kautsky the Renegade', as well as K. Marx, 'The Civil War in France', all in *A Handbook of Marxism* (New York: International Publishers, 1935).
2. Marx and Lenin were pointing to the need for an all-encompassing analysis. In relation to this study, then, any analysis of the effect of 'international factors' must be applied not only to the state and internal social forces, but also to those movements that act in the name of the oppressed. This requires that the activities/pressures of representatives of capital – both international and domestic – should be applied specifically to the ANC.
3. Proof of this can clearly be seen in the majority of post-colonial 'liberations' in Africa, for example, Algeria, Ghana, Guinea-Bissau, Kenya, Zimbabwe, etc.

1 The Formative Years

1. Quoted in Fine and Davis (1990, p. 52).
2. This process of increased racial and class polarisation and exploitation is excellently chronicled and analysed in Simons and Simons (1983).
3. It is important to note that it was during the war years, in 1943, that the ANC Women's League was formed. Although the ANC had committed itself to a policy of equal status for women in the organisation, the all-male ANC leadership kept the Women's League under its thumb and the League's functions were extremely limited despite women having been in the forefront of many active campaigns. See Walker (1982).
4. In this light the historical development of South Africa has been labelled 'racial capitalism'. For extended discussions on this, see Legassick (1974, pp. 253–91).
5. See McKinley (1986). Also Danaher (1985).
6. See for example the 'official' and 'unofficial' histories of the ANC in Meli (1988) and Holland (1989) respectively.
7. Lodge (1983, p. 72) makes this point and it is confirmed by one of those who was on the sub-committee, Ben Turok (Ben Turok, interview with author, October 1992). There was also the effect of state repression that took its toll on the ability of the Alliance to canvass and involve large numbers of people. Fine and Davis (1990) have also argued that the Charter was not widely debated, and the

process as a whole was more of a successful political mobilising tool than anything else (pp. 139–47). At any rate, it is obvious that the claims of mass involvement are at least exaggerated.

2 National Liberation of a Special Type (1960–75)

1. Cited in Callinicos (1986, p. 23).
2. See ANC, *Submit or Fight: 30 Years of Umkhonto we Sizwe* (Johannesburg: ANC Political Education Section, 1991); Kasrils (1993); and Mandela (1990).
3. Many of the main figures in MK as well as in the external mission of the ANC were members of the SACP. On the MK side these included Joe Slovo, Govan Mbeki, Ahmed Kathrada, Dennis Goldberg and Jack Hodgson. Of the external mission complement, Tennyson Makiwane, Mzwai Piliso and Moses Mabhida were Party members.
4. This was the essence of the ANC's later justifications for the decision to turn to armed struggle contained in their 1969 'Strategy and Tactics' document adopted at the Morogoro Conference in Tanzania.
5. The word *laager* is from the Afrikaans and was used to describe the ox-wagon formation that the early Afrikaner pioneers made when faced with attack from hostile enemies.
6. This collection of activists so influenced, along with the Mandela generation, were to become known as the 'Islanders', so called because of their 'schooling' on Robben Island. Many of these 'Islanders' were to play major roles in the ANC after their release, and particularly after its unbanning in 1990.

3 From Soweto to Kabwe (1976–84)

1. Slovo (1976, pp. 148–9).
2. Oliver Tambo, 'Support our People until Power is Restored to Them', Address to the Plenary Meeting of the General Assembly (United Nations), New York, 26 October 1976, in Reddy (1991, p. 70).
3. Cited in Karis (1983, p. 191).
4. The term 'securocrats' refers to high ranking military and police personnel who came to occupy centre-stage in the government of P.W. Botha, and sidelined political officials in the decision- and policy-making process.
5. The largest and most infamous was Quatro (named after a notorious Johannesburg prison known as No. 4), a camp situated in northern Angola. It was only after the ANC's unbanning that news of Quatro and the subsequent mutinies came to light. See Ellis and Sechaba (1992, ch. 6) as well as the journal *Searchlight South Africa* 5 (1990). These events took place between 1981 and 1984.
6. To date, more detailed information on the mutinies and subsequent responses is not available, hence the reliance on Ellis and Sechaba, an account that is generally considered to be the most accurate information available.

4 The Politics of Ungovernability: Insurrectionary Hopes and Strategic Realities (1988–89)

1. ANC NEC Statement, April 1985, p. 2.
2. The Vaal triangle is so called for a cluster of townships to the east of Johannesburg. The larger townships include Sebokeng, Thokoza, and Kathlehong. The Vaal triangle had a heavy concentration of industrial workers and unemployed shack dwellers situated in the industrial heartland of South Africa.
3. The 'necklace' was one of the methods used to punish those considered enemies of the 'struggle'. It consisted of placing a car tyre around the victim's neck, filling it with gasoline and then setting it alight. Although Winnie Mandela was not an official leader of the UDF, her stature as a tireless resister of apartheid and wife of Nelson Mandela, afforded her statements added weight and importance. Much of the UDF leadership condemned her statement, but in reality all she was doing was giving verbal expression to a component of the logic of a strategy of ungovernability.
4. The term derived its meaning from combining the words comrade and tsotsi (meaning criminal).
5. SACP (1963, pp. 3–18).
6. From 1985 to 1988 the number of MK attacks inside the country increased dramatically. For example, in 1988 MK launched 281 attacks, almost five times more than in 1984 (See Barrell, 1990, ch. 4).
7. There had already begun a sizeable exodus of conservative Afrikaners from the National Party in the 1987 elections, and the failure in Angola only exacerbated the sense among many Afrikaners that the National Party could no longer guarantee their political and economic security.

5 Fourth Pillar, Fifth Column: The Internationalisation of the Struggle

1. The fourth pillar refers to one of four stated aims of the ANC's liberation struggle – the international isolation of the apartheid regime (it usually appeared in written documents as the last of the four aims).
2. Cited in Holland (1989, p. 230).
3. For examples of this from 'observers', see Holland (1989) and Magubane (1989). 'Participant' examples, besides Meli (1988), are to be found throughout liberation movement literature after February 1990.
4. See 'U.S. Assistance to South Africa Report', State Department Fact Sheet, 22 April 1986.
5. The only analysis that attempts to make a similar argument can be found in Paul Trewhela, 'Financial Sanctions and the future of South Africa', *Searchlight South Africa*, No. 4 (February, 1990) pp. 13–32.

6. The SACP continued to affirm the leading role of the working class. For example, in *Umsebenzi* Vol. 6, No. 1 (First Quarter, 1990), under the heading 'No Let-up on Sanctions' the SACP stated that 'the most reliable motive [for supporting sanctions] is class solidarity based on common interests as members of an exploited class. Socialists regard this as a cardinal principal of working class politics' (p. 20).

7. The Harare Declaration had been drawn up by the ANC and first submitted to a summit of Heads of State of the African Frontline states in Lusaka on 10 August 1989. After having been unanimously adopted there, it was then tabled and adopted at a conference of Heads of State of the Organisation of African Unity's Ad-Hoc Committee on Southern Africa in Harare on 21 August 1989.

6 Returning Home: The Strategy and Practice of Accommodation (1990–93)

1. Cited in Marx and Engels (1984, p. 281). Marx was not referring to reformism *per se*, but fundamental reform of existing economic and political systems.

2. Other leaders of the Interim Group included UDF notables Popo Molefe, Patrick 'Terror' Lekota and Raymond Suttner.

3. See Joe Slovo, 'Has Socialism Failed?', *African Communist* (Second Quarter, 1990) pp. 25–51. In an attempt to assess critically past 'wrongs' and 'rescue' socialists and socialism, Slovo argued that Soviet-style 'socialism' lacked democracy. While Slovo's contribution rightly highlighted the lack of democracy practised in the USSR and Eastern Europe (albeit after decades of SACP abuse for anyone daring to question the infallibility of Soviet-style 'socialism'), the practical direction it pointed to was one of further accommodation to the interests of the apartheid state and capital.

4. Alliance allegations of a 'third force' were continually dismissed throughout the negotiation period. Although the apartheid state-appointed Harms Commission Report (late 1990) found that the apartheid state's Civil Cooperation Bureau (CCB) seemed to be behind a series of death-squad killings and other potential cases of apartheid-related violence, it was not until 1996 that conclusive 'proof' confirmed the Alliance position.

5. 'Simon' is a pseudonym. The interviewee had recently returned from exile and was, at the time, an active ANC member and resident of Soweto.

6. Winnie Mandela had been charged (and eventually acquitted) by the state with being an accomplice to the murder of a black teenage activist named Stompie (allegedly carried out by a group of her 'bodyguards' calling themselves the 'Mandela Football Club'). The trial, which dragged on for several months, divided much of the ANC leadership and general membership, and produced a highly publicised separation between Nelson and Winnie.

7. Also see ANC Department of Economic Policy, 'Discussion Document: Nationalisation' (Cape Town: Center for Development Studies, n.d.).

8. The author, who visited these prisoners, personally saw several of these letters.

9. The 'Leipzig option' refers to the quasi-insurrectionary uprising that took place in Leipzig, Germany during the upheavals in the then East Germany prior to the overthrow of the 'communist' government in the early 1990s.

10. In the next issue of the *African Communist* (Fourth Quarter, 1992), several articles appeared that took issue with Slovo, including contributions from the late SACP stalwart Harry Gwala and ANC NEC member Pallo Jordan. There was also a great deal of expressed opposition from within the organised working class, which led to a COSATU-initiated 'Reconstruction Accord', which would bind a future government to the provision of 'basic needs' and hopefully ensure the interests of the working class. See COSATU, 'Reconstruction Accord', 4th Draft, internal Alliance document, 1993.

Conclusion

1. The 'far right' in this case denotes the white right (although Inkhata was also considered to pose a substantial threat), which consisted of an amazing range of groups from the 'respectable' Conservative Party, to the neo-nazi AWB, to small 'ultra-right' organisations like the World Apartheid Movement.

2. These would include (among others), the FLN of Algeria, the PAIGC of Guinea-Bissau/Cape Verde, ZANU/ZAPU of Zimbabwe, the MPLA of Angola and the FSLN of Nicaragua. As in the case of the ANC, there were no doubt many within the movements that did not share this perspective, but reference here is to the leadership.

3. The ANC's Strategic Perspectives Document, under the sub-heading 'Phases of the Democratic Revolution', stated:

   Our strategic perspective should take into account that the democratic revolution – for the attainment of majority rule – will proceed in various phases. Our possibilities relevant to each phase should not be pursued in a manner that produces defeats later because of a failure to recognise the dialectical interconnection between various phases.

4. For examples see the last two issues (Nos 95 and 96) of *Work in Progress* as well as Saul (1991).

5. The RDP – initially a COSATU-inspired programme – is designed to wed an ANC government to a more radical commitment to policies that would address the needs of workers and the unemployed. Since its first draft in late 1993, many of the most important issues addressed in the RDP (such as housing) have literally been hijacked by representatives of big capital. All such 'social forces' (mentioned in the text), no doubt fully recognise the benefits of being fellow-travellers in reconstructing and developing the new South Africa.

6. In early 1996 the government unveiled a 'new' economic strategy –
called the 'Growth, Equality and Redistribution' macro-economic
strategy – which commits the government to a growth-first, monetarist
and trickle-down programme. Despite its misleading title, it represents
a clear abandonment of any radical restructuring and redistribution
in favour of the majority of South Africans while enhancing the
already massive economic power of domestic and international
monopoly capital.

References

This bibliography includes a selected list of books and articles consulted in the course of work on this study. For purposes of clarity this bibliography also includes separate lists of primary sources and unpublished papers and mimeos

Africa Research Centre (1989) *The Sanctions Weapon* (Cape Town: Buchu Books)

Alexander, Neville (1993) *Some Are More Equal Than Others: Essays on the Transition in South Africa* (Cape Town: Buchu Books)

Amin, Samir (1977) *Imperialism and Unequal Development* (New York: Monthly Review Press)

—— (1993) 'SA in the Global Economic System', *Work in Progress*, No. 87

Arendt, Hannah (1965) *On Revolution* (New York: Viking Press)

Astrow, Andrew (1983) *Zimbabwe: Revolution that Lost its Way?* (London: Zed Press)

Aya, R. (1979) 'Theories of Revolution Reconsidered', *Theory and Society*, No. 8

Barrell, Howard (1985) 'ANC Prepares for Consultative Conference', *Work in Progress*, No. 35

—— (1990) *MK: The ANC's Armed Struggle* (London: Penguin Books)

Baskin, Jeremy (1991) *Striking Back: A History of the Congress of South African Trade Unions* (Johannesburg: Ravan Press)

Benson, Mary (1966) *Struggle for a Birthright* (Harmondsworth: Penguin Books)

—— (ed.) (1986) *Nelson Mandela: The Man and the Movement* (New York: W.W. Norton & Company)

Biko, Steve (1986) *I Write What I Like*, ed. Aelred Stubbs (New York: Harper & Row)

Bond, Patrick (1991) *Commanding Heights and Community Control: New Economics for a New South Africa* (Johannesburg: Ravan Press)

Bundy, Colin (1982) 'The Emergence and Decline of a South African Peasantry', in Martin Murray (ed.) *South African Capitalism and Black Political Opposition* (Cambridge, MA: Schenkman Publishing Company)

—— (1987) 'History, Revolution and South Africa', *Transformation*, No. 4

—— (1989) 'Around Which Corner?: Revolutionary theory and contemporary South Africa', *Transformation*, No. 8

Bunting, Brian (1986) *The Rise of the South African Reich* (London: International Defense and Aid Fund)

Burns, Emile (ed.) (1935) *A Handbook of Marxism* (New York: International Publishers)

Callinicos, Alex (1986) 'Marxism and Revolution in South Africa', *International Socialism*, No. 31

—— (1988) *South Africa: Between Reform and Revolution* (London: Bookmarks)

—— (1992) *Between Apartheid and Capitalism: Conversations with South African Socialists* (London: Bookmarks)

Carolus, Cheryl (1989) 'Nothing Less than the Transfer of Power', *New Era*, Vol. 4, No. 3 (October)

Chomsky, Noam and Edward Herman (1979) *The Washington Connection and Third World Fascism* (Boston, MA: South End Press)

Coker, Christopher (1986) *The United States and South Africa (1968–1985): Constructive Engagement and its Critics* (Durham, NC: Duke University Press)

Crocker, Chester (1980/81) 'South Africa: Strategy for Change', *Foreign Affairs*, No. 59

Cronin, Jeremy (1992) 'The Boat, the Tap and the Leipzig Way', *African Communist*, No. 130

Danaher, Kevin (1985) *The Political Economy of United States Policy Towards South Africa* (Boulder, CO: Westview Press)

Davidson, Basil, Joe Slovo and Anthony Wilkinson (1976) *Southern Africa: The New Politics of Revolution* (New York: Penguin Books)

Davies, Rob (1988) 'Nationalisation, Socialisation and the Freedom Charter', in John Suckling (ed.) *After Apartheid: Renewal of the South African Economy* (London: James Currey)

Davis, Stephen (1987) *Apartheid's Rebels: Inside South Africa's Hidden War* (New Haven, CT: Yale University Press)

de Braganca, Aquino and Immanuel Wallerstein (eds) (1982) *The African Liberation Reader*, Vols 2 and 3 (London: Zed Press)

Deutschmann, David (ed.) (1987) *Che Guevara and the Cuban Revolution: Writings and Speeches of Ernesto Che Guevara* (Sydney: Pathfinder Press)

Ellis, Stephen and Tsepo Sechaba (1992) *Comrades against Apartheid: The ANC and the South African Communist Party in Exile* (London: James Currey)

Esterhuyse, Willie (1990) 'The ANC and Negotiations', in W. Esterhuyse and A. Nel (eds) *The ANC and its Leaders* (Cape Town: Tafelburg)

Fatton, Robert (1984a) 'The African National Congress in South Africa: The Limitations of a Revolutionary Strategy', *Canadian Journal of African Studies*, No. 18

—— (1984b) 'The Reagan Foreign Policy Toward South Africa: The Ideology of the New Cold War', *The African Studies Review*, No. 27

—— (1986) *Black Consciousness in South Africa* (Albany, NY: State University Press)

Feit, Edward (1962) *South Africa: The Dynamics of the African National Congress* (London: Oxford University Press)

Fine, Robert (1992) 'Civil Society Theory and the Politics of Transition in South Africa', *Review of African Political Economy*, No. 55

Fine, Robert and Dennis Davis (1990) *Beyond Apartheid, Labour and Liberation in South Africa* (Johannesburg: Ravan Press)

Frank, Andre Gunder (1969) *Capitalism and Underdevelopment in Latin America: Historical Studies of Chile and Brazil* (New York: Monthly Review Press)

—— (1979) *Dependent Accumulation and Under-development* (New York: Monthly Review Press)

Friedman, Stephen (1987) 'The Struggle within the Struggle: South African Resistance Strategies', *Transformation*, No. 3

Geras, Norman (1990) *Discourses of Extremity: Radical Ethics and Post-Marxist Extravagances* (London: Verso)

Gramsci, Antonio (1971) *Selections From Prison Notebooks*, ed. Quinton Hoare (London: Lawrence and Wishart)

Hani, Chris (1991) 'Waiting for the next order', *Mayibuye*, Vol. 2, No. 3

Hanlon, Joseph (1986) *Apartheid's Second Front: South Africa's War against its Neighbours* (New York: Penguin Books)

—— (1987) *The Sanctions Handbook* (New York: Penguin Books)

Harris, Laurence (1993) 'South Africa's Economic and Social Transformation: From "No Middle Road" to "No Alternative"', *Review of African Political Economy*, No. 57

Hemson, Dave (1978) 'Trade Unionism and the Struggle for Liberation in South Africa', *Capital and Class*, No. 6

Hirson, Baruch (1979) *Year of Fire, Year of Ash* (London: Zed Press)

—— (1990) *Yours for the Union: Class and Community Struggles in South Africa 1930–1947* (London: Zed Books)

Hobson J.A. (1988) *Imperialism: A Study*, 3rd edition (London: Unwin Hyman)

Holland, Heidi (1989) *The Struggle: A History of the African National Congress* (London: Grafton Books)

Independent Expert Study Group (1989) *South Africa: The Sanctions Report* (London: Penguin Books)

Innes, Duncan (1984) *Anglo American and the Rise of Modern South Africa* (London: Heinemann)

Institute for Black Research (1993) *The Codesa File: Negotiating a Non-Racial Democracy in South Africa* (Durban: Madiba Publishers)

Jeeves, Alan (1982) 'The Control of Migratory Labour on the South African Gold Mines in the era of Kruger and Milner', in M. Murray (ed.) *South African Capitalism and Black Political Opposition* (Cambridge, MA: Schenkman Publishing Company)

Johns, Sheridan (1973) 'Obstacles to Guerilla Warfare: A South African Case Study', *Journal of Modern African Studies*, Vol. 11, No. 2

Johns, Sheridan and R. Hunt Davis (eds) (1991) *Mandela, Tambo and the African National Congress: The Struggle against Apartheid, 1948–1990* (New York: Oxford University Press)

Jordan, Pallo (1990) 'Crisis of Conscience in the SACP', *South African Labour Bulletin*, Vol. 15, No. 3

Kaplan, B.H. (1978) *Socialist Change in the Capitalist World Economy* (Beverly Hills, CA: Sage Publications)

Kaplan, D.E. (1982) 'The Politics of Industrial Protection in South Africa', in M. Murray (ed.) *South African Capitalism and Black Political Opposition* (Cambridge, MA: Schenkman Publishing Company)

Karis, Thomas (1983) 'Competing for Hearts and Minds in South Africa', in T. Callaghy (ed.) *Southern Africa* (New York: Praeger)

Kasrils, Ronnie (1990) 'Kasrils on Umkhonto', *Work in Progress*, No. 68

—— (1993) *Armed and Dangerous: My Undercover Struggle against Apartheid* (Oxford: Heinemann Educational)

—— and Khuzwayo (1991) 'Mass Struggle is the Key', *Work in Progress*, No. 72

Laurence, Patrick (1990) *Death Squads. Apartheid's Secret Weapon* (London: Penguin Forum Series)

Legassick, Martin (1974) 'South Africa: Capital Accumulation and Violence', *Economy and Society*, No. 3

Lenin, V.I. (1932) *Imperialism: Highest Stage of Capitalism* (New York: International Publishers)

—— (1935) 'The Proletarian Revolution and Kautsky the Renegade', in Emile Burns (ed.) *A Handbook of Marxism* (New York: International Publishers)

—— (1947) *Revolutionary Proletariat and the Right of Nations to Self-Determination* (Moscow: Progress Publishers)

—— (1950) *'Left-Wing' Communism, an Infantile Disorder* (Moscow: Progress Publishers)

—— (1969) *What is to be Done?* (New York: International Publishers)

—— (1977) *Collected Works*, Vols 6, 20 (London: Lawrence and Wishart)

—— (1977) 'Letters on Tactics', in *Collected Works*, Vol. 6 (London: Lawrence and Wishart)

Lerumo, A. (1980) *Fifty Fighting Years: The Communist Party of South Africa (1921–1971)* (London: Inkululeko Publishers)

Lipton, Merle (1985) *Capitalism & Apartheid: South Africa, 1910–1986* (Cape Town: David Philip Publishers)

Lodge, Tom (1983) *Black Politics in South Africa since 1945* (Johannesburg: Ravan Press)

—— (1983/84) 'The ANC in South Africa, 1976–83: Guerilla War and Armed Propaganda', *Journal of Contemporary African Studies*, Vol. 3, Nos 1/2

—— (1985) 'The Second Consultative Conference of the African National Congress', *South Africa International*, Vol. 16, No. 2

—— (1987a) 'State Power and the Politics of Resistance', *Work in Progress*, Nos 50/51

—— (1987b) 'The African National Congress after the Kabwe Conference', in G. Moss and I. Obery (eds) *South African Review* 4 (Johannesburg: Ravan Press)

—— (1988) 'State of Exile: The African National Congress of South Africa, 1976–86', in P. Frankel and M. Swilling (eds) *State, Resistance and Change in South Africa* (London: Croom Helm)

—— and Bill Nasson (1991) *All Here and Now: Black Politics in South Africa in the 1980s* (Cape Town: David Philip Publishers)

Luthuli, Albert (1978) *Let My People Go* (Glasgow: Fontana Books)

Magubane, Bernard (1981) 'Imperialism and the National Liberation Struggles in Southern Africa', in David Wiley and Allen Isaacman (eds) *Southern Africa: Society, Economy and Liberation* (Lansing, MI: Michigan State University Press)

—— (1989) *South Africa: From Soweto to Uitenhage* (Trenton, NJ: Africa World Press)

Makgetla, Neva (1985) 'Why We Call for Sanctions', *Sechaba* (September)

Mandela, Nelson (1983) *No Easy Walk to Freedom* (London: Heinemann)

Marais, Hein (1991) 'Political Progress May Undo the Glue Unifying the ANC', *Business Day* (18 September)

Marcum, John (1978) *The Angolan Revolution: Exile Politics and Guerilla Warfare (1962–76)*, Vol. 2 (Cambridge, MA: MIT Press)

Martin, David and Phyllis Johnson (eds) (1986) *Frontline Southern Africa: Destructive Engagement* (New York: Four Walls Eight Windows)

Marx, Anthony (1992) *Lessons of Struggle: South African Internal Opposition, 1960–1990* (Cape Town: Oxford University Press)

Marx, Karl (1935) 'The Civil War in France', in Emile Burns (ed.) *A Handbook of Marxism* (New York: International Publishers)

—— (1970) *A Contribution to the Critique of Political Economy*, ed. Maurice Dobb (New York: International Publishers)

—— (1973) *Grundrisse* (Harmondsworth: UK Penguin Books)

—— and Frederick Engels (1972) *On Colonialism* (New York: International Publishers)

—— (1984) *Collected Works*, Vol. 6 (Moscow: Progress Publishers)

Mashinini, Alex (1986) 'Dual Power and the Creation of People's Committees', *Sechaba* (April)

Mayekiso, Mzwanele (1993) 'The Legacy of "Ungovernability"', *Southern African Review of Books*, Vol. 5, No. 6

Mbeki, Govan (1984) *The Peasants' Revolt* (London: International Defence and Aid Fund)

—— (1992) *The Struggle for Liberation in South Africa* (Cape Town: David Philip Publishers)

McKinley, Dale (1994) 'Class and Democracy in the Struggle For Socialism: A Reply to the "Structural Reformers" and "Radical Democrats"', *Links*, No. 3

Milkman, Ruth (1982) 'Apartheid, Economic Growth and United States Foreign Policy in South Africa', in Martin Murray (ed.) *South African Capitalism and Black Political Opposition* (Cambridge, MA: Schenkman Publishing Company)

Mkatashingo (1991) '"Letter to the Editors", The ANC Conference: From Kabwe to Johannesburg', *Searchlight South Africa*, No. 6

Mokoena, Kenneth (ed.) (1993) *South Africa and the United States: The Declassified History* (New York: The Free Press)

Morris, Mike (n.d.) 'Redistributive Reform', *Indicator SA* (Issue Focus)

Moss, Glenn and Ingrid Obery (eds) (1986) *South African Review 3* (Johannesburg: Ravan Press)

—— (eds) (1988) *South African Review 5* (Johannesburg: Ravan Press)

—— (eds) (1991) *South African Review 6: From Red Friday to Codesa* (Johannesburg: Ravan Press)

Murray, Martin (ed.) (1982) *South African Capitalism and Black Political Opposition* (Cambridge, MA: Schenkman Publishing Company)

—— (1994) *Revolution Deferred: The Painful Birth of Post-Apartheid South Africa* (London: Verso)

Mzala, Comrade (1986) 'Building People's War', *Sechaba* (September)

—— (1988) *Gatsha Buthelezi: Chief with a Double Agenda* (London: Zed Press)

Nolutshungu, Sam (1982) *Changing South Africa: Political Considerations* (New York: Africana Publishing Company)

Nzimande, Blade (1992) 'Let Us Take the People with Us', *African Communist*, No. 131

Ovenden, Keith and Tony Cole (1989) *Apartheid and International Finance: A Program for Change* (Victoria, Australia: Penguin Books)

Oxall, Ivor, Tony Bennet and David Booth (eds) (1975) *Beyond the Sociology of Development: Economy and Society in Latin America and Africa* (London: Routledge)

Padayachee, Vishnu (1987) 'Apartheid South Africa and the International Monetary Fund', *Transformation*, No. 3

Pampallis, John (1991) *Foundations of the New South Africa* (London: Zed Press)

Pauw, Jacques (1991) *In the Heart of the Whore* (Johannesburg: Southern Books)

Pillay, Devan (1992) 'Fighting the Violence: Mass Action or Mass Struggle?', *Work in Progress*, No. 83

Pomeroy, William (1968) *Guerilla Warfare & Marxism* (New York: International Publishers)

—— (1986) *Apartheid, Imperialism and African Freedom* (New York: International Publishers)

Reddy, E.S. (ed.) (1991) *Oliver Tambo: Apartheid and the International Community* (London: Kliptown Books)

Rejai, Mostafa (1977) *The Comparative Study of Revolutionary Strategy* (New York: David McKay Co.)

Relly, Gavin (1986) '"The Perversity of Sanctions", Address given to the South Africa–Britain Trade Association, 26 August', supplement to *Optima*, Vol. 34, No. 3

Roux, Edward (1966) *Time Longer Than Rope: A History of the Black Man's Struggle for Freedom in South Africa* (Madison, WI: University of Wisconsin Press)

Ruiters, Greg and Rupert Taylor (1990) 'Organise or Die', *Work in Progress*, Nos 70/71 (November/December)

SACP (1987) 'National Liberation and socialism', *Work in Progress*, Nos 50/51

Saul, John (1991) 'South Africa: between "Barbarism" and "Structural Reform"', *New Left Review*, No. 188

Saul, John and Stephen Gelb (1986) *The Crisis in South Africa: Class Defense, Class Revolution* (New York: Monthly Review Press)

Schire, Robert (1991) *Adapt or Die: The End of White Politics in South Africa* (New York: Ford Foundation)

Seidman, Ann and Neva Seidman Makgetla (1980) *Outposts of Monopoly Capitalism: Southern Africa in the Changing Global Economy* (London: Zed Press)

Simons, J. and R. Simons (1983) *Class and Colour in South Africa 1850–1950* (London: International Defense and Aid Fund)

Skocpol, Theda (1979) *States and Social Revolutions: A Comparative Analysis of France, Russia and China* (Cambridge: Cambridge University Press)

Skocpol, Theda and E.K. Trimberger (1978) 'Revolution and the World Historical Development of Capitalism', in B.H. Kaplan (ed.) *Socialist Change in the Capitalist World Economy* (Beverly Hills, CA: Sage Publications)

Slovo, Joe (1976) 'South Africa – No Middle Road', in Basil Davidson, David Wilkinson and Joe Slovo (eds) *Southern Africa: The New Politics of Revolution* (Harmondsworth: Penguin Books)

—— (1990) 'Has Socialism Failed?', *African Communist*, No. 121

—— (1992) 'Negotiations: What Room for Compromise?', *African Communist*, No. 130

Sparks, Allister (1991) 'The ANC pulls together', *Africa South*, No. 13.

State Department Report to Congress (1987) 'Communist Influence in South Africa', *Transformation*, No. 3

Stockwell, John (1978) *In Search of Enemies* (New York: W.W. Norton & Company)

Study Commission on United States Policy Toward South Africa (1981) *South Africa: Time Running Out* (Berkeley, CA: University of California Press)

Ticktin, Hillel (1991) *The Politics of Race Discrimination in South Africa* (London: Pluto Press)

Trewhela, Paul (1990) 'Financial Sanctions and the Future of South Africa', *Searchlight South Africa*, No. 4

—— (1991) 'The AFL–CIO and the Trade Unions in South Africa', *Searchlight South Africa*, No. 2

Trotsky, Leon (1967) *On Black Nationalism and Self-Determination* (New York: Pathfinder Press)

—— (1972) *Leon Trotsky Speaks*, ed. Sarah Lovell (New York: Pathfinder Press)

Turok, Ben (1974) 'South Africa: The Search for a Strategy', in R. Miliband and J. Saville (eds) *Socialist Register 1973* (New York: Monthly Review Press)

—— (ed.) (1980) *Revolutionary Thought in the Twentieth Century* (London: Zed Press)

United Democratic Front (1985) 'Convention Alliance', *Isizwe*, Vol. 1, No. 1

von Holdt, Karl (1990) 'Insurrection, Negotiation, and "War of Position"', *South African Labour Bulletin*, Vol. 15, No. 3

Walker, Cheryl (1982) *Women and Resistance in South Africa* (Cape Town: David Philip Publishers)

Wallerstein, Immanuel (1979) *The Capitalist World Economy: Essays* (Cambridge: Cambridge University Press)

—— (1983) 'The Integration of the National Liberation Movement in the Field of International Liberation', *Contemporary Marxism*, No. 6

Walshe, Peter (1971) *The Rise of African Nationalism in South Africa: The African National Congress (1912–1952)* (Los Angeles: University of California Press)

Wilson, Francis (1971) 'Farming, 1866–1966', in M. Wilson and L. Thompson (eds) *The Oxford History of South Africa*, Vol. 2 (Oxford: Oxford University Press)

Wolpe, Harold (1975) 'The Theory of Internal Colonialism: the South African Case', in Ivor Oxaal, Tony Bennett and David Booth (eds) *Beyond the Sociology of Development* (London: Routledge)

—— (1990) *Race, Class and the Apartheid State* (London: James Currey)

Worden, Nigel (1994) *The Making of Modern South Africa: Conquest, Segregation and Apartheid* (Oxford: Blackwell Publishers)

Primary Sources

African National Congress Documents

(n.d.) 'Discussion Document: Nationalisation' (Cape Town: ANC Department of Economic Policy – Centre for Development Studies)

(1958) ANC Constitution

(1969) Strategy and Tactics of the ANC (London: ANC)

(1983a) 'Circular to all ANC missions and Solidarity organisations' (November) (Lusaka: ANC)

(1983) '"What is to be Done?", Statement of ANC NEC on January 8' (Lusaka: ANC)

(1984a) 'ANC NEC Statement' (March) (Lusaka: ANC)

(1984b) '"Clarion Call to all Opponents of Apartheid", Address by Oliver Tambo to the Greater London Council' (21 March) (Lusaka: ANC)

(1985) '"The Future is Within Our Grasp", Statement of the National Executive Committee of the ANC' (April) (Lusaka: ANC)

(1986) 'Sanctions Will Help Defeat Apartheid' (London: ANC)

(1987a) 'Documents of the ANC Conference, "People's of the World United Against Apartheid for a Democratic South Africa", 1–4 December' (Lusaka: ANC)

(1987b) 'NEC Statement, 8 January' (Lusaka: ANC)

(1987c) 'Statement of the National Executive Committee of the African National Congress on the Question of Negotiations' (October) (Lusaka: ANC)

(1988) 'ANC NEC Statement, August 17' (Lusaka: ANC)

(1990a) 'Advance to National Democracy: Report on the ANC National Consultative Conference, 14–16 December' (Johannesburg: ANC)

(1990b) 'The Road to Peace' (June) (Johannesburg: ANC Department of Political Education)

(1991a) 'ANC Position on the Land Question – Discussion Document for the National Conference' (March) (Johannesburg: ANC)

(1991b) 'ANC National Conference Report, July 1991' (Johannesburg: ANC Department of Information and Publicity)

(1991c) 'Discussion Document: Constitutional Principles and Structures for a Democratic South Africa' (Cape Town: ANC Constitutional Committee – Centre for Development Studies)

(1991d) 'Submit or Fight: 30 Years of Umkhonto we Sizwe' (Johannesburg: ANC Political Education Section)

(1991e) 'Tasks of the ANC in the Present Period', ANC internal discussion document (Johannesburg: ANC)

(1991f) '"Year of Mass Action for the Transfer of Power to the People", Statement of the National Executive Committee on the occasion of the 79th anniversary of the African National Congress, January 8' (Johannesburg: ANC)

(1992a) 'ANC Policy Guidelines for a Democratic South Africa', internal draft discussion document (Johannesburg: ANC)

(1992b) '"Year of Democratic Elections for a Constituent Assembly", Statement of the National Executive Committee on the occasion of the 80th anniversary of the African National Congress, January 8' (Johannesburg: ANC)

(1992c) 'Negotiations: A Strategic Perspective', as adopted by the National Executive Committee of the African National Congress, 25 November (Institute for Black Research, 1993, pp. 348–61)

(1993) 'ANC NEC Statement, 8 January' (Johannesburg: ANC)

(1994) 'The Reconstruction and Development Programme' (Johannesburg: ANC – Umanyano Publications)

South African Communist Party Documents

(1963) 'Statement of the Central Committee of the South African Communist Party', *African Communist* (April/June)

(1981) South African Communists Speak (London: Inkululeko Publications)

(1985) 'Statement of the Central Committee of the South African Communist Party', *African Communist* (Second Quarter)

(1986a) 'Does Insurrection Need People's War?', *Umsebenzi*, Vol. 2, No. 1

(1986b) 'The Reformist Role of Workerism', *Umsebenzi*, Vol. 2, No. 1

(1989) 'Manifesto of the South African Communist Party. The Path to Power' *Umsebenzi*, Vol. 5, No. 2

(1992) 'Manifesto of the South African Communist Party. Building Worker's Power for Democratic Change' (Johannesburg: Umsebenzi Publications)

Additional Primary Sources

Congress of South African Trade Unions (1992) 'Documentation: Economic Policy Conference' (Johannesburg: COSATU)

de Klerk, F.W. (1990) 'Address by State President F.W. de Klerk at the opening of the Second Session of the Ninth Parliament of the Republic of South Africa, Friday 2 February 1990 (S.A. Embassy, London, media release)

ELTSA (1989) 'South Africa's Debt Crisis'. A background paper prepared for the No Debt Rescheduling Campaign by End Loans to Southern Africa (London)

Karis, Thomas and Gwendolen Carter (1972, 1973, 1977) *From Protest to Challenge: A Documentary History of African Politics in South Africa 1882–1964*, 4 vols (Stanford, CA: Hoover Institution Press)

Mandela, Nelson (1990) *The Struggle is My Life* (New York: Pathfinder Press)

Mayibuye Centre Microfilm Collection (Cape Town: University of the Western Cape)

Meli, Francis (1988) *South Africa Belongs to Us: A History of the ANC* (Harare: Zimbabwe Publishing House)

South African Congress of Trade Unions (1978) 'Political Report of the General Secretary to the National Executive Committee of SACTU' (January)

South African History Archives Collection (Johannesburg)

United Democratic Front (1985) 'Declaration of the United Democratic Front' (August)

Unpublished Papers and Mimeos

Appolis, John and Susan Tilly (1993) 'Discussion Article on the Reconstruction Accord', unpublished paper (Johannesburg)

Bond, Patrick (1990) 'The Politics of Financial Sanctions', unpublished paper (Harare)

Burkett, Paul (1993) 'Social-Democratic Imperialism: Requiem for an Analytical Marxist', unpublished paper (Bloomington, IN)

—— (1994) 'Which Way Now?: Socialism or Capitalizing Socialist Priorities?', unpublished paper (Bloomington, IN)

Dorabji, Elena V. (1983) 'South African National Congress: Change from Non-Violence to Sabotage between 1952 and 1964', PhD dissertation (Ann Arbor, MI: University Microfilms)

Friedland, Elaine (1980) 'A Comparative Study of the Development of Revolutinary Nationalism in Southern Africa – FRELIMO and the ANC', PhD dissertation (Ann Arbor, MI: University Microfilms)

Habib, Adam (n.d.) 'The Theory of the South African Revolution: "Colonialism of a Special Type" and the National Democratic Revolution', unpublished paper (Johannesburg)

IRRC (1989) 'U.S. Banks and South Africa. Analysis L', mimeo (Washington DC)

Legassick, Martin and Dave Hemson (1976) 'Foreign Investment and the Reproduction of Racial Capitalism, An Anti-Apartheid Movement pamphlet', mimeo (London)

Lewis, Jack (1991) '"Mixed Economy" – Illusions of Reformism', Paper presented to the Africa Seminar of the Centre for African Studies, University of Cape Town (Cape Town)

Lodge, Tom (1994) 'The African National Congress Comes Home', African Studies Seminar paper, University of Witswatersrand (Johannesburg)

Maharaj, Mac (1988) 'Internal Determinants of Pretoria's Present Foreign Policy', Paper presented to Seminar in Memory of Aquino de Braganca and Ruth First, Centro de Estudos Africanos, Universidade Eduardo Mondlane (Maputo, Mozambique)

McKinley, Dale (1986) 'United States Foreign Policy Towards South Africa (1969–1985): Continuity and Contradiction', MA thesis, Department of Political Science, University of North Carolina–Chapel Hill

Schmidt, Elizabeth (1987) 'United Nations Sanctions and South Africa: Lessons from the Case of Southern Rhodesia', United Nations Centre Against Apartheid, Notes and Documents (New York)

Suttner, Raymond (1991) 'One Year of an Unbanned ANC. The Road Ahead' (Johannesburg: ANC Internal Department of Political Education paper)

—— (1993) 'Negotiations – Site of Struggle or Site of Surrender?', Internal ANC discussion paper (Johannesburg)

'The Worker's Movement and SACTU: A Struggle for Marxist Policies' (n.d.) mimeo

Tumahole, Justice (1993) 'A Contribution to the Strategic Perspective Debate', unpublished paper (Johannesburg)

Index

Index by Auriol Griffith-Jones